COLLECTING
JAPANESE
ANTIQUES

COLLECTING JAPANESE ANTIQUES

ALISTAIR SETON

TUTTLE

Published by Tuttle Publishing, an imprint
of Periplus Editions (HK) Ltd.

www.tuttlepublishing.com

Copyright ©2004 Alistair Seton

ISBN 978 4 8053 1122 6 pb
ISBN 978 0 8048 2094 3 hc

Distributed by

North America, Latin America & Europe
Tuttle Publishing
364 Innovation Drive
North Clarendon, VT 05759-9436 U.S.A.
Tel: 1 (802) 773-8930
Fax: 1 (802) 773-6993
info@tuttlepublishing.com
www.tuttlepublishing.com

Japan
Tuttle Publishing
Yaekari Building, 3rd Floor
5-4-12 Osaki
Shinagawa-ku
Tokyo 141 0032
Tel: (81) 3 5437-0171
Fax: (81) 3 5437-0755
tuttle-sales@gol.com

Asia Pacific
Berkeley Books Pte Ltd,
61 Tai Seng Avenue, #02-12
Singapore 534167
Tel: (65) 6280-1330
Fax: (65) 6280-6290
inquiries@periplus.com.sg
www.periplus.com

hc 10 09 08 07 06 05 04   5 4 3 2 1
pb 14 13 12 11 10   5 4 3 2 1

Printed in Singapore

TUTTLE PUBLISHING® is a registered
trademark of Tuttle Publishing, a division
of Periplus Editions (HK) Ltd.

Page 2 *Ishō ningyō* of Hotei, one of
seven lucky gods, early 19th c., ht 13 in
(33 cm). Rosen Collection. Photo courtesy Akanezumiya.

Page 3 Two *hibachi* (braziers), hand-
painted blue-and-white porcelain,
early 20th c. Photo courtesy Kurofune
Antiques.

This page *Netsuke*, ivory, of Seiōbo
("queen mother of the west") holding
a peach branch, anon., 18th c., 5 in (13
cm). Photo courtesy Sagemonoya.

Page 5 Gold lacquer and metal inlay
five-case *inrō*, angel and aristocrat
design, signed Koma Kyūhaku and
Hamano Kuzui; *roiro* and gold writing
box *netsuke* and peach *ojime* in wood
and shell inlay. Author's Collection.

CONTENTS

JAPAN'S ART HERITAGE

Art in Japan has a long and glorious history that compares with that of any civilization. This book is *not* a history of Japanese art. After a short survey of many interesting features, old things are looked at with a collector's eye and an awareness that most ancient masterpieces are in temples and museums and are therefore unavailable for purchase. Yet those areas also deserve to be known and studied, like those to which collectors gravitate either from choice or fate. The aim is to provide some historical background, then examples and analysis in areas where collecting is feasible. Information and advice is offered to the would-be collector or the simply curious.

Japan as a Storehouse

Japan is a kind of attic of ancient art. Ever since the building of the Shōsōin Imperial Storehouse in AD 756, leaders have deliberately preserved as much as possible of the past. One might say that a *kura* (a fireproof storehouse built near the houses of the wealthy) is an apt image for the whole country. Wars may have devastated Kyoto, and the "flowers of Edo" (a term used to describe terrible, dangerous city fires) burnt much that was beautiful in Tokyo, but much too has been kept or rebuilt. The scope of the Imperial Collections attests to the desire to retain good things from the past. Even after taking power from the court, the shōgun (military dictators) proved they were men of culture, building on past achievements and patronizing great artists. Temples and shrines also played a vital role in preserving treasures against time, theft, and fire.

An astonishing number of Heian era (794–1185) and older objects remain in the safekeeping of shrines and temples, and important families. Much is owed to the generations of priests and others who kept the flame alive. They could have made their own lives easier by selling off the past but managed against the odds to save a great artistic and cultural heritage for the future.

Hōryūji, a great seventh-century temple near Nara, is particularly famous for hoarding the past. A thirteenth-century catalogue reveals its secret vaults hold 1.32 tons of gold, 10,000 copper roofing tiles, and 30,000 mirrors. Although the location is known, the priests will not open the vaults. Tradition says Regent Shōtoku Taishi (574–622) ordered them not to be opened for a thousand years after his death, and only later if finances were dire. Hōryūji has faced penury but still the priests refused to open them to historians. According to Ishikawa Takeshi in *Traditions: A Thousand Years of Japanese Beauty*, it sold thousands of the pagodas given by Empress Shōtoku in 770; each contains a mystic prayer verse or *dharani*. These mystic prayer verses are the oldest extant printed matter in the world. Hōryūji still has 40,300 of the 100,000 bequeathed!

Another statue of Kan'non (Goddess of Mercy) had been kept sealed since the seventh century in the nearby Hall of Dreams (Yumedono), rumored to be on the site where Shōtoku Taishi lived, which may have caused the secrecy, and he may be the model. In the late nineteenth century, the famous American aesthetician Ernest Fenollosa, sculptor Kanō Tessai, and art theorist Okakura

Fig. 1

ca. 1000 BC	300 BC	AD 300	710
			AD 593
JOMON CULTURE	**YAYOI ERA**	**KOFUN ERA**	**ASUKA PERIOD**
Era known after rope marks on earthenware pots with strange ornate tops; some use of lacquer. Hunting and gathering society.	Iron and bronze tools smelted, wet rice farming started. Hierarchical society.	*Kofun* = burial mound, like 5th c. Emperor Nintoku's key-hole-shaped grave, 1,600 ft (486 m) long with three moats. Later co-existed with Asuka era. Introduction of Buddhism 538 or 552.	Buddhism and Sino culture seeped in earlier but now imposing temples built, centralizing laws made under Regent Shōtoku. Literacy spread among leaders and clergy.

Fig. 1 Jōmon (rope-patterned) earthen jar, mid-Jōmon era, ca. 3000 BC, ht 9 in (23 cm), excavated at Chō-jagahara, Ni'igata Prefecture. Jar has characteristic raised, flame-like relief lines and animal designs. Photo courtesy Kyoto National Museum.

Fig. 2 Fourteen *dōtaku* (ceremonial bells) and seven halberd heads from Sakuragaoka-chō, Kobe, mid-Yayoi era (AD 100?), designated National Treasures, max. ht of *dō-taku* 25 in (63 cm), halberds 11 in (28 cm) long. Photo courtesy Kobe City Museum.

Fig. 2

Tenshin demanded to be shown it. They were refused but persisted though the priests said the heavens would open. Tenshin got in and was greeted by 1,200 years of stale air but the three found a superb Asuka-era (seventh-century) Kan'non in perfect condition, as related by Fenollosa in his *Epochs of Chinese and Japanese Art*.

Spareness, Asymmetry, and Stylization

From Heian times, when sexual morality was less important than aesthetic taste, Japanese art has tended to avoid depicting the ugly or vulgar and to concentrate instead on nature rather than man, the symbolic rather than the realistic. The major thrust is *yūgen* or refined, near mystical elegance, showing an almost feminine sensibility. It has delighted in flowing lines and irregular shapes, eschewing the square or symmetrical, and has accepted that art is impermanent—hence the attraction of three-day cherry petals and *mono no aware* (the pathos of transience). Typical materials seem fragile to a Western eye: wooden temples, bark roofs, mud walls, straw mat floors, translucent paper windows, paper scrolls and prints.

Telling concepts include an aim for simplicity (words like *wabi* and *sabi*, meaning austere simplicity with a hint of loneliness), or *shibui* (restrained, avoiding the showy), as well as an uncluttered or empty space (*ma*) which allows the onlooker to add his own something. Interestingly, *ma* is applied in all the arts, even music where silence may convey more than sound, and in comic theater where timing is everything.

Spareness is valued in the look of a page and the brevity of a poem (hence *haiku*'s mere three lines and *waka*'s five), an understated teahouse, unsculpted stone lantern, or a flowerless pebble garden. Artists aim to achieve such technical mastery that they can create a work with *muga* (no gap between the imaginative moment and the accomplishment), whereas a lesser artist feels some veil, some hesitation between his wish and the fulfillment.

Stylization (*yōshiki-ka*) and stratification into hierarchies have always been important. If you look at people in older art or later woodblock prints (*ukiyo-e*), they tend to have the traditional "hook nose and line mouth," so reveal no individuality or realism. In a way "a woman is a woman," without thinking about what makes her unique. At the same time, artists have been categorized since around 1600 in ascending order of honor into *hōkyō*, *hōgen*, and *hōin*, so signatures on scrolls may start, for example, with *hōgen*. Titles like *tenka-ichi* ("best under heaven" but really "best in Japan") and *jō-ichi* ("best locksmith") have also been given.

Interesting technical facets include the way space is broken up in paintings by clouds to delineate areas (we see this in screens, where distant Mt Fuji could be "near" Kyoto) or form a general background, and in furniture by *chigaidana*, interrupted shelving, where a shelf ends halfway with a descent to a higher/lower level, with an S-bend or angular corner. A desire for subdued simplicity has co-existed with sumptuous gold screens and lacquerware, the Golden Phoenix Pavilion at Uji, and the gaudy, overdecorated temples of Nikkō (though this is not the core of Japan's aesthetic tradition as the temples were erected for political reasons).

An excellent statement of Japan's aesthetic is *Tsurezuregusa* (Essays in Idleness), written about 1330 by Yoshida Kenkō. He praises the under- or overripe, the no longer perfect, the frayed but good quality scroll over the new. He also believed that it was beginnings and ends that are interesting. Modern Japanese have forgotten the latter but continue to enjoy the bud more than the flower. In all, the keen aesthetic sense in Japan's ferocious yet graceful ancient sculptures, medieval swords, sixteenth-century screens, castles, Edo era *netsuke* and *inrō* (*netsuke* are *obi* or belt counter-balancers and *inrō* little drawered boxes dangling from the *obi*) and kimono is a major component of mankind's artistic heritage.

794

1185

NARA PERIOD

Nara copied Chinese capital; great trade/cultural contact with Asia in Tempyō era (729–49). Emperors, Fuji-wara family, and Buddhist priests fought. Tōdaiji Great Buddha completed in 752; cost trampled peasants (some fled farms or revolted). Artistic flowering.

HEIAN ERA

Early Heian era (till mid-9th c.)

Emperors proclaimed land ownership and bureaucracy. Kokinshū poem anthology starred Ono no Komachi and Ariwara no Narihira. Diary tradition started by Ki no Tsurayuki.

Mid Heian era (till 1050)

Chinese influence waned. Great lady writers Murasaki Shikibu (*The Tale of Genji*), Sei Shōnagon (*Pillow Book*), and Izumi Shikibu (poems).

Late Heian era

Landowners' power increased. Retired emperors took back power from Fujiwaras but central control weakened, increasing military and Taira family control. Taira/Minamoto clans fought. Taira defeated at Dan-no-Ura (1185). Minamoto Yoritomo (1147–99) founded Kamakura shōgunate in east. Zen Buddhism gradually spread from priests to warriors.

Unknown and Speculative Early History

The first examples found in Japan of works embodying man's desire for beauty are the recently found ca. 15,000-year-old pottery shards from the Jōmon period (13000–300 BC)—as old as anywhere on earth. At that time, Japan was probably still linked to Korea and Russia. When the Ice Age ended, the Japan Sea rose, leaving Japan an archipelago. Naturally, many Jōmon pieces are incomplete, but fascinate us with their weird crowns or arabesque tracery and rope-induced markings. The law says that newly excavated items belong to the state and Jōmon pieces are not readily available to collectors, but pieces do reach the market and recent shows (for example, at the British Museum in 2001) have revealed how wonderful these pots are with their incredible crowns (Fig. 1).

The Jōmon gave way to the Yayoi era (300 BC–AD 300) when pots became restrained, but more typical are the *dōtaku* or ceremonial bronze bells (Fig. 2). The Kofun era (AD 300–710) is named after its massive grave mounds or tumuli. Earlier human sacrifices were replaced by earthenware servants, soldiers, and animals to accompany the rich on their journey into the next life: these fascinating figures are called *haniwa* (Fig. 3). They appear goofy to some and charming to others in current reproductions. The many extant bronze mirrors had magical powers (they could see spirits) as well as practical use in checking one's coiffure or make-up.

Imperial burial mounds are huge and their secrets carefully hidden by the Imperial Household Agency. The *Wajinden* section on Japan of the third-century Chinese history *Wei Zhi* tells us about the shaman queen Himiko of Yamatai being buried in a tumulus, along with 100 male and female servants. The 80 acre (32.3 hectare) burial mound of Nintoku (r. 395–427) is very impressive from the air. Important secrets will be revealed when permission is finally given for archaeologists to enter this vast grave south of Osaka.

From the sixth century, a cultural tide flowed in from Korea and China, bringing knowledge of Buddhism and advanced arts of the two countries, like metalworking, textile weaving, and government. Later, a quarter of the courtiers were said to be Koreans.

The First Buddhist Masterpieces

There was considerable opposition to Buddhism from nationalists but this did not halt the completion of the first large temples by the end of the sixth century (Shiten'nōji in 593; Asukadera in 596; Wakakusadera ca. 607, near Osaka). Architects and artists started from Korean and Chinese originals. We know that Shiba Tori,

Fig. 3

Fig. 3 Male *haniwa*, Kofun era (6th c.), ht 29 1/2 in (75 cm), excavated at Waki-ya, Gunma Prefecture. The figure has a sedge hat, *mizura* hair style, short sword, and hoe. Other *haniwa* were warriors, female shamans, and farmers with tools or weapons. Photo courtesy Kyoto National Museum.

Fig. 4 Mandala of Dakini-ten, Muromachi era (ca. 1500), hanging scroll, color on silk, 32 x 16 in (81 x 41 cm). Taman Collection. Photo courtesy Osaka Municipal Museum of Art.

1185	1333	1392	1573	1603
KAMAKURA PERIOD	**MUROMACHI (OR ASHIKAGA) PERIOD**		**MOMOYAMA PERIOD**	**EDO OR TOKUGAWA PERIOD**

KAMAKURA PERIOD	MUROMACHI (OR ASHIKAGA) PERIOD	MOMOYAMA PERIOD	EDO OR TOKUGAWA PERIOD
Military rule from Kamakura; Hōjō family ascendant. Fujiwara Teika compiled Hyakunin Isshu (100 *waka* by 100 poets (ca. 1236). Mongol invasions of 1274–81 repelled by "divine wind" (*kamikaze*). Spread of Pure Land Buddhism; Hōnen, Shinran, and Nichiren popularize Buddhism. 13th c. war tale *Heike Monogatari*.	Nambokuchō era 1333–92. Disputing (dual) emperors, north and south. Ashikaga family shōguns in power till Ōnin War (1467–77), then puppets (often of the Hosokawas) causing the endless wars of the Sengoku era 1482–1573. Later Ashigawas were greater art patrons than warriors.	Oda Nobunaga (1534–82) took power in Kyoto from 1568, gradually (and cruelly) extending power till death by treachery. Toyotomi Hideyoshi (1536–98) accepted as leader by emperor in 1585, completed unification in 1591. Failed in two invasions of Korea. Great artistic achievements; famous for gold screens.	Tokugawa Ieyasu (1543–1616) won great Sekigahara Battle in 1600, defeating Hideyoshi's son Hidenori: officially ruler from 1603. Son Hidetada made shōgun 1605 but Ieyasu worked strategically to eliminate Hidenori (destroyed Ōsaka Castle in 1615); laid framework for long Tokugawa rule. Genroku (1688-1704) era: cultural/economic swelling of townsmen's culture (e.g. *ukiyo-e* and theater; Chikamatsu wrote plays, Bashō wrote *haiku*. Saikaku wrote social stories. Ogata Kenzan/Kōrin brothers and Ninsei potted

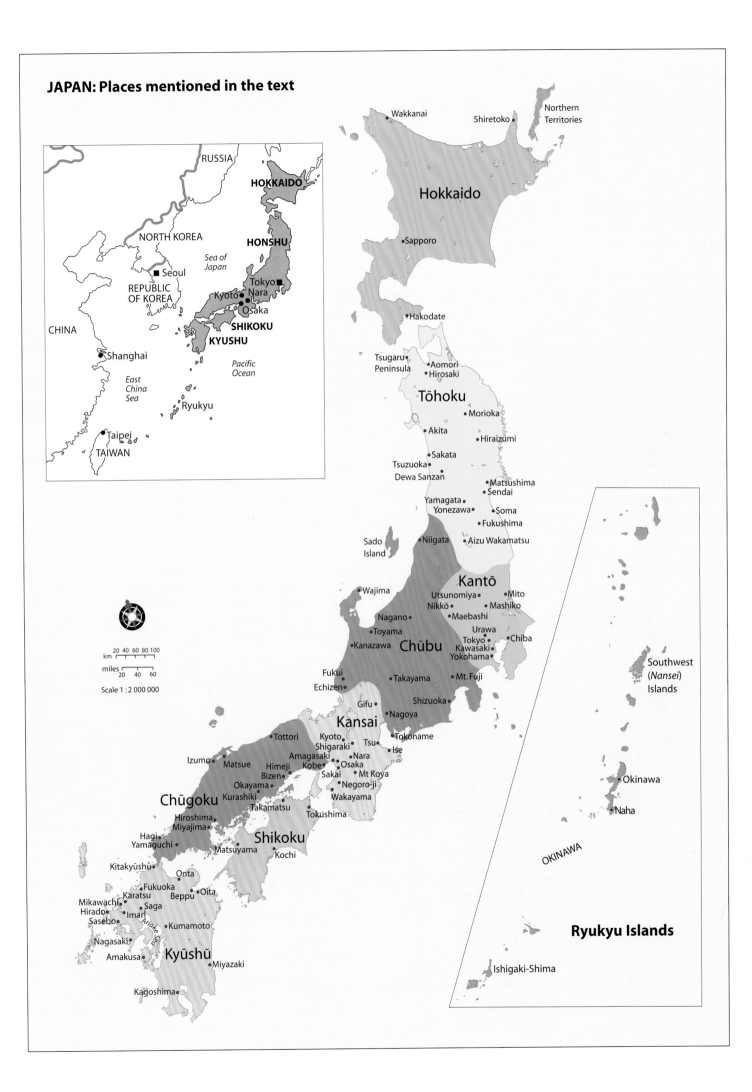

JAPAN: Places mentioned in the text

RUSSIA

HOKKAIDO

NORTH KOREA

Sea of Japan

HONSHU

Seoul

REPUBLIC OF KOREA

Tokyo
Kyoto • Nara
Osaka

SHIKOKU

CHINA

KYUSHU

Shanghai

East China Sea

Pacific Ocean

Ryukyu

Taipei

TAIWAN

Wakkanai
Shiretoko
Northern Territories

Hokkaido

Sapporo

Hakodate

Tsugaru Peninsula
Aomori
Hirosaki

Tōhoku

Morioka

Akita

Hiraizumi

Sakata

Tsuzuoka
Dewa Sanzan

Matsushima
Sendai

Yamagata
Yonezawa
Soma

Fukushima

Sado Island

Niigata
Aizu Wakamatsu

Kantō

Wajima
Utsunomiya
Mito
Nikkō
Mashiko
Nagano
Maebashi
Toyama
Urawa
Kanazawa
Chūbu
Tokyo
Chiba
Kawasaki
Yokohama

Fukui
Takayama
Mt. Fuji
Echizen
Shizuoka

Gifu
Nagoya
Kansai
Kyoto
Tottori
Shigaraki
Tsu
Nara
Amagasaki
Ise
Izumo
Matsue
Kobe
Himeji
Osaka
Tokoname
Bizen
Sakai
Mt Kōya
Okayama
Negoro-ji
Kurashiki
Wakayama
Chūgoku
Takamatsu
Hiroshima
Tokushima
Miyajima
Shikoku
Hagi
Matsuyama
Yamaguchi
Kochi
Kitakyūshū
Onta
Fukuoka
Oita
Mikawachi
Karatsu
Beppu
Hirado
Saga
Sasebo
Imari
Ariake
Nagasaki
Kumamoto
Amakusa
Kyūshū
Miyazaki
Kagoshima

Southwest (*Nansei*) Islands

Okinawa

Naha

OKINAWA

Ryukyu Islands

Ishigaki-Shima

km 20 40 60 80 100
miles 20 40 60
Scale 1 : 2 000 000

Changing Taste

Taste changes with time. When I was young, everybody looked down on Victorian furniture because it was "heavy and in bad taste." Nowadays, it is back in fashion. This pattern recurs, particularly with the styles of periods too recent for detachment. The artists and works of whole periods may be tarred with the feathers that should stick only to some artists who did inferior work, or used poor materials. For a time people laughed at Art Deco, Grandma Moses, and Lowrie. Now they are worshipped. Meiji art and handicrafts were condemned a generation ago, but now the good parts grace great exhibitions. Taste is fluid in food, clothes, and art.

When foreigners first come to live in Japan, they look around with their old eyes and old ideas, buying things older hands avoid. That is part of the learning process. If you buy nothing you regret later, you must be very controlled or tight with money—certainly not adventurous! But it is usually a good idea to wait a little until, by dint of eating carrots, you can see better in the netherworld.

Taste is determined by time and acclimatization, contact, and knowledge. What you buy in the first few weeks off the plane and what you collect years later differ. You are changed by time spent in a new environment and contact with people and things there. Knowledge of the new way of life you pick up talking, seeing, and living with things lends a new perspective, a new pair of eyes. This is the great thing about learning new languages, or adventuresome journeys: you grow and acquire a new persona. You notice more subtle color variations, textures, and materials you had missed. You understand why people prefer the pre-chemical colors of older textiles and porcelain, and accept the marks of the years on often-washed indigo fabric or child-banged chests. The patina of age seems worth paying for. The eye seeks something different, no longer novelty for its own sake. The eye becomes stricter, or "higher," as they say in Japanese.

To a certain extent, this process is inevitable, but the pace at which it occurs can be slowed or speeded up. The more you search around and keep a lookout for the interesting and beautiful, the faster your eye gets attuned to the new aesthetic, the new hierarchy of values. If you find that nothing much appeals to you, you are free to keep the old eyes and leave Japan the way you came—though aesthetically poorer. In Japan, you can get to know a unique sense of beauty. Cut off from outside influences, the cultural traits already here in the sixteenth century deepened and within a seamless social fabric developed independently. Many forms of art reached a perfection and originality unmatched elsewhere. Welcome to Xanadu and Kublai Khan's easterly stately pleasure dome!

An Occupational Disease

Those who spend decades here as collectors or dealers get jaded and appreciate less sharply the antiques around them. They may remember the wonderful things they saw twenty years before and seek the same quality. Though natural, this path leads to disappointment, like a fisherman recounting the fish that got away. "Distance lending enchantment," growing discernment, the vanishing into museums of many of the nicest things (making fewer available for later private purchase), and occasional theft, breakage, or vandalism are behind this occupational disease. Old hands see the past in rosy tints as they were younger then and prices were lower—and fewer collectors had money—just like them!

If they say there is nothing left worth buying—a common complaint about fairs at Heiwajima or Kyoto, Osaka, New York, or London, there is truth in it—for those people. But readers of this book should realize that each age finds things to collect because the spirit of the age evolves, and generations die, leaving estates formed earlier with other tastes. The adventurous or imaginative will find things to collect long after some say nothing of interest remains. Morita Akio, former head of Sony, had the money to collect Impressionists but instead collected old Victrolas and other phonograph-type things. An investment banker, Richard Weston, came to Tokyo around 1983. He was taken with *inrō* and *netsuke* (ornaments suspended from the belt) and collected them. He soon assembled a collection good enough to be honored with an exhibition at Christie's in 1995, accompanied by an excellent book. If he had been dissuaded by older collectors, he would never have started on such a venture. We would all be the poorer.

Others have collected *inrō* and thought there was little out there unrecorded, but Weston had an imaginative insight: one can assemble the full trio of *netsuke*, *ojime* (bead fastener), and *inrō* from singletons found separately, provided one is lucky and matches them with taste. In this way he built a valuable collection. These separate objects were made by craftsmen skilled in various trades. The sets were made to go together but the motifs were not necessarily the same. By doing the process in the reverse order, Weston found natural-looking pairings. Similarly, Robert Fleischel of Sagemonoya, Tokyo, found danglers hidden for 39 years in an attic.

The Restoration Debate

Most people agree that older objects acquire a certain extra quality through the years, and that this patina is valuable and should be retained if possible. In Japan it is called *aji*. If everything was kept as carefully as the Imperial treasures in the Shōsōin Imperial Storehouse—taken out only occasionally for airing and checking, never subject to wear and tear from puppies and drinks, kept safely off the ground away from humidity, and guarded against theft—then

Fig. 12   **Fig. 13**

pottery festival and wanted a focus during the fair. Tourism is a common reason for new museums!

Endowing a museum takes a king's ransom. Owners often sell their collection cheaply to an existing museum or donate it as a named collection. You might think museums would jump at a donation and they may, if it includes things they wanted anyway. In fact, donations are often refused, as the items may be outside the museum's scope, or the museum may not have the space or budget. This seems Irish, but if a museum operates at a loss already and would have to devote resources to accept the new acquisition, like space and staff, then it makes sense to refuse.

Pleasures of Collecting

Gardening provides mental stimulation and a link with our farming past. Sowing, hoeing, weeding, and watching seedlings grow enchant—like children or pets. Weather and bugs cause setbacks, while forgetting to water or a week away may kill treasured plants. Collecting has similar rewards but no worrying diseases, while travel may widen a collection, unlike neglecting a garden. Instead of careful attention to the weather, fertilizer, or fumigant, collectors should be dogs—sniff along roads for the scent of your quarry, and chew at books on your chosen field! Buy a few decorative things or others for kitchen use to see what appeals. Only if you are intrigued, should you start on the full adventure!

The pleasures of collecting are bound up with creation, like a gardener. Normally, we non-artists rarely feel the thrill of creation. But putting different works side by side creates links between them not seen before. Perhaps one attractive doll and then another share some characteristic you saw elsewhere. When you put all three together, you may see another link—you are creating a new order. You may also create new knowledge. If some special dolls usually bear no mark, but while rummaging through a store, you find one in an original box which has *kanji* on it, which the curio seller identifies as being, for example, "Tanaka of Osaka," you may have stumbled on knowledge which is important for telling a future collector and scholar about the creators of these dolls. Do not throw the box away: you are a scholar now!

Decorating your house creatively appeals—a new corner, wall display, or piece of furniture. We enjoy visitors looking at our buys—a talking point, a point of departure for a dinner party. As in walking a dog, you soon find antique-friends. Decorating creates a world, even if just a bedroom corner. If you keep a few dolls or saké cups from each city you visit by the dressing table, that spot serves as a log of your time in Japan, especially if you record the date and who you were with.

Some people get a thrill from showing how many examples of an item they find. If a friend has more, then still feel proud and perhaps find more, but only if you can use more, or want a full collection. Remember Buckminster Fuller's dictum that all things have an optimal length or breadth: "more may be less." Perhaps it is preferable to cull and buy better pieces to outdo your friend.

The spirit of the hunt can entice. There is nothing more satisfying than sorting through piles in secondhand stores for the print you wanted! As hunter, you survey your collection and your prey's terrain, adding *un je ne sais quoi* to your life. Perhaps you are in marketing and need to hit sales targets. But at the office you rely on a whole team, while the product itself may have little appeal for you personally. It can be hard to love toothpaste or floppy disks!

An Antidote to the Rat Race

If interested, you buy without sales literature or ads in the antique world—and no spiel. A shrine seller may pipe an advanced message: "Gaijin-san. Good plates, very cheap!" That smiling call is better than TV ads or a PR talk. If you go back, (s)he and the others will remember you—unlike your TV. As individualists, dealers are not prepackaged but quirky. They do not commute daily in suits like robots but are often kind. When phones finally started working after the 1995 quake, I got calls from dealers everywhere. Many in far-off Kantō or Kyūshū only knew me as a man coming once a year or so to look, yet they tried for weeks to get in touch with me, out of sympathy. I felt blessed.

A teacher for decades, I love explaining. Bringing varied things together, imposing some order, and explaining them is more satisfying than socially rewarding activities like balancing the books or preparing for class. In some deeper sense, it is more "me."

Some collectors love pictures by famous painters or works once owned by stars, reveling in the prestige—certainly one attraction. Individualists prefer things which are unknown, but might become popular—palpable adventure! Finally, it is fun to have round you things of value at least in the longer term, not in a deposit box. Scrooge missed something: counting gold coins is for mugs. Having attractive, things round you is more fun, more natural than living among landlord- or firm-chosen goods. Even a bird chooses the materials she builds her nest with—"That feather looks nice and I think I'll try some of this down and that moss looks nice." Why not take flight like her?

Fig. 25

SCREENS AND SCROLLS

For centuries Japanese screens, along with swords and lacquer, have been considered to excel those of any other nation. The Chinese invented screens, but by the sixteenth century the Japanese had surpassed their teachers and brought screens to a stage where the artistic aspects and technical mastery (the way the various panels were joined flexibly but lightly with paper hinges, and panel surrounds were abandoned to provide an unbroken painting surface) made them the gift of choice for highly ranked beneficiaries. Many were sent to Spain, Mexico, and Rome with delegations to please the powers that were back then. The Chinese also imported them. By their very presence, screens tend to overawe. Unlike many Japanese arts, they are painted on a formidable scale. A standard pair of six-panel screens measures 24 feet (7.3 meters) wide and provides a huge, continuous surface on which to paint heroic-sized pictures which can vie with the proportions loved by Louis XIV at Versailles. Screens, *fusuma* (sliding doors), hanging scrolls (*kakejiku* or *kakemono*), fans, and hand-rolled scrolls (*e-makimono*) have been the main vehicles for Japan's fine art for centuries. To a certain extent, the format is interchangeable. Screens or *fusuma* may be cut down and made into hanging scrolls if there is a change of mind or architecture, or a part gets damaged. Hand scrolls can be turned into individual prints, while fans are often pasted on screens. Josetsu's early masterpiece, "Catching a Catfish with a Gourd," was originally a partitioning screen but is now a hanging scroll.

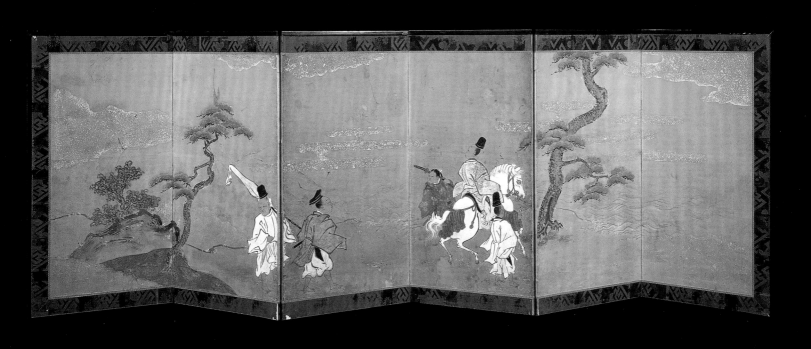

Early History of Screens

The Chinese first made screens in the third century BC. Screens came to Japan in the seventh century (the earliest reference is AD 686 in *Nihon Shoki*). By 756, Tōdaiji Temple in Nara stocked a hundred, on both secular and religious themes.

In the Heian era (794–1185), a distinction began to be made between *Yamato-e* (non-religious pictures with Japanese themes and style, such as cherries, maples, birds, and seasonal changes), and *Kara-e* (those inspired by China). Japanese have tended to prefer practical objects even in art. Screens and paintings on doors served the purpose of separating space—dividing a room, keeping out drafts, forming a backdrop to a religious ceremony, or partitioning off a storage space. There was little room for "art for art's sake." Art had to work!

Screens and poets were closely connected at the Heian court. Poems were composed specifically for screens and scrolls, often depicting verdant hills in the changing seasons, or genre scenes. Most *Yamato-e* paintings were made for the court, while religious institutions kept commissioning pictures of saints and more especially mandalas, which explain Buddhist theories in graphic ways. Although few paintings prior to the twelfth century remain, the religious hold Buddhism exerted for centuries weakened from then on, though tea ceremony addicts and followers of Zen Buddhism, with its call for precepts and pithy epithets, widened the scope of screens and scrolls, adding dogma and priestly portraits.

Structural Improvements to Screens

Murase Miyeko states in *Masterpieces of Japanese Screen Painting: The American Collection* that in eighth-century screens "each of the six panels was originally surrounded by a silk border of brilliant red, and the panels were tied to one another at the top and bottom with colored leather thongs or silken cords. Each panel was regarded as a separate, independent pictorial unit, as well as a component of a single decorative piece…. This ancient method of joining screen panels was gradually modified. In the early thirteenth century, panels were arranged so that the brocaded border surrounded every two panels, rather than each individual one.

"The final solution to the problem of this still unsatisfactory format appears to have been achieved in the early fourteenth century, producing the format which is still in use today. The leather or silk cords that had once linked the *byōbu* (i.e. screen) panels were abandoned. In their place, strips of paper were pasted, horizontally, from the front of one panel to the back of the next, forming hinges. The strips alternated with other strips of paper affixed to the panels in the reverse direction."

To explain a little more clearly, these paper hinges provide contact and stability, much like tendons in the human body. When you stretch your leg, its shape changes as the tendons are pulled

Fig. 27

straight by the muscles or compressed by others. You can see the slight ripple of the paper hinge on a screen through the covering material. The alternating direction of the hinges provides stability; if one strip of paper gets weaker, the next one above and below should still hold and give the strength and flexibility needed. The strips of paper are covered with gold or white paper where visible and the same material as the back, where invisible. The new brocade frame is visible at the top and bottom of each panel, and at the far left and far right sides of the screen. As Murase says, "this technical innovation at last made it possible to display a continuous and unified composition in a screen painting."

Now artists could execute sweeping, uninterrupted images on the surface of both screens, achieving an unprecedented aesthetic level of room decoration. Some later artists designed dramatic, even epic subjects like towering tree trunks rising out of sight or the whole panoply of the seasons. Others concentrated on smaller-scale subjects like autumn grasses, ducks or kimono on racks.

According to Liza Hyde, "though screens originated in China, they reached their apex in Japan, perhaps because the Japanese had fewer interior walls (and mobile ones appealed to them); the Chinese liked monumental walls hung with scrolls and large, lacquered wooden screens better. In English they were known as Coromandel (as they were brought out through the Straits of Coromandel). Paper hinges would not suit these heavy pieces. Korean screens later took after the Japanese and used paper hinges."

(Previous page) Fig. 26 Machi-Kanō School, "Tales of Ise," six-panel screen, *sumi* (Indian ink) and color on paper, 17th c., 2 ft 6 in x 8 ft 6 in (76 cm x 2.6 m). Photo courtesy Liza Hyde.

Fig. 27 Kyōno, "Archery Lesson" (mother teaching son), two-panel screen, *sumi* and color on paper, c. 1920, 5 ft 7 in x 6 ft (1.7 x 1.8 m). Photo courtesy Liza Hyde.

Fig. 28 Anon., "Cranes" (detail), six-panel screen, *sumi* and color on paper with gold clouds, 18th c., 5 ft 6½ in x 12 ft (1.7 x 3.6 m). Photo courtesy Liza Hyde.

Fig. 29 Kō Hōgen, 15th descendant of Kanō Motonobu, "Shishi" (lions) six-panel screen, 19th c. (Edo), 6 ft x 12 ft 3 in (1.8 x 3.6 m). Photo courtesy Liza Hyde.

Fig. 28

Gold Screens

Gilded screen painting appeared in the fourteenth century. The entire surface was covered with paper-thin sheets of gold leaf. These found good markets in neighboring countries. Hyde adds: "There was a sharp increase in the domestic demand for gold screens in the mid-fifteenth century. They were used at funeral rites in Buddhist temples, and in the homes of cultivated men as convenient backdrops against which hanging scrolls of painting and calligraphy could be displayed."

Initially, the gilded panels remained undecorated, but soon they came to be painted in ink or lavish colors. Gold flakes of varying hues were sprinkled onto gilded surfaces, and gold was used along with ink and colors. The total effect was dazzling. The Momoyama screens made at the end of the sixteenth century and early in the seventeenth were the most famous. *Daimyō* developed a mania for building castles with extravagant interiors featuring gold screens. These screens reflected light in dark rooms, making the rooms look warmer and also more magnificent. Masters painted bold, impressive images against shimmering gold or silver grounds. In these surroundings, monochrome ink screens created a special ambience. Hazy mist and water landscapes form a metaphysical world of concentration, meditation and poetry.

Fig. 29

Fig. 30

Fig. 31

Fig. 32

Fig. 33a, b

Common Screen Subjects

Landscapes (*sansui*) are the best known subjects in scrolls. You may be surprised to learn that Japan's scenery really can look like the traditional mist-shrouded hills with prominent pines portrayed in screens, especially after rain in June. The great Sesshū Tōyō (1420–1506) may have been inspired by Chinese predecessors, but such scenes also exist here (see Fig. 5).

Rakuchū rakugai. This is a variant of the above but shows genre scenes set in Kyoto or neighboring places. Clouds often divide the different scenes and localities—a little mystifying until you understand the convention.

Four seasons (*shiki*). The seasons typical of Kyoto were taken as true of all Japan and portrayed in pairs or fours: spring/summer on one and autumn/winter on the other.

Flower and bird (*kachō*) combinations. These are also extremely popular as the images are pretty and contain no harshness. Traditional groupings are the pine, bamboo, and flowering plum (*shōchikubai*), sparrows in a bamboo grove, or Mt Fuji, a hawk, and eggplant (the three best dreams of the New Year). Cranes and turtles imply long life. Birds of prey suggest aggressiveness. Graceful flowers like peonies have felicitous associations with feminine beauty and aristocracy. Standing pines and clinging wisteria metaphorically suggest men and women together.

Tagasode. Literally "whose clothes," these depict kimono on an *ikō* or kimono rack, with other familiar clothes or objects, such as cages, parrots, or braziers perfuming sleeves (Fig. 49a, b).

Mythical or traditional themes. The Seven Lucky Gods, heroes such as Benkei and Yoshitsune fighting on Kyoto's Gojō Bridge, or the battle between two famous women's carts (reflecting deep jealousy and disappointed love), are areas where a knowledge of Japanese history, myth, and religion makes a big difference to one's appreciation of a screen.

Religious motifs. Common are pictures of temples, statues of Kan'non, and *raigō* or pictures welcoming believers into the Western Paradise (these relieved the suffering of those about to die, as they were reassured that a place in heaven awaited them).

Zen images. These usually depict hairy or weird figures of great élan and expressiveness, such as Daruma, the inseparable smiling pair of Kanzan and Jittoku, or ascetics. Some have a cartoon-like quality or represent kabuki figures. I suspect these images face instantaneous love or loathing, unlike other forms.

Military scenes. Many were made to urge boys to grow up into brave soldiers and were exhibited on the former Boys' Day (May 5th). At the time of the Sino-Japanese (1894–5) and Russo-Japanese Wars (1904–5), and during the military period before and during World War II, there was a resurgence of patriotism expressed in many ways.

Domestic scenes. Views of people at a tea house, scholars in a garden, or Chinese boys (*karako*) with funny shaved heads, perhaps chasing butterflies, are common.

Portraits. These are rare compared to the West, though those of priests are commoner. Often posthumous, they remind followers of his teachings. The tradition requires typical and idealistic images, not realistic portraits (see Fig. 7).

Fig. 30 Anon., "Pines, Water and Wisteria," six-panel screen, *sumi* and color on heavily embossed gold, late 17th c., 5 ft 8 in x 12 ft 2 in (1.7 x 3.7 m). Photo courtesy Liza Hyde.

Fig. 31 Anon., "Hawks," one of a pair of six-panel screens, ink and color, late 16–17th c., each 5 ft 6 in x 12 ft 2 in (1.7 x 3.7 m), purchased in Japan in 1933 from Fujita by Paul Theodore Frankl and from his estate. Photo courtesy Liza Hyde.

Fig. 32 Anon., "Morning Glories, Vines and Grasses," six-panel screen, mineral colors on gold leaf, early 18th c., 5 ft 8½ in x 12 ft (1.7 m x 3.6 m). Photo courtesy Liza Hyde.

Fig. 33a, b Seikō, "Corn Festival" (details), pair of two-panel screens, ink and color, 20th c., each 5 ft 5½ in x 6 ft 2 in (1.7 m x 1.9 m). Photo courtesy Liza Hyde.

Fig. 34

Fig. 35

Fig. 36

Screens with Calligraphy

Works with nothing but writing are perhaps the hardest to get to like, but are also very exotic as they are entirely outside Westerners' cultural realm. They are abundant and cheaper than other subjects (many are still made for monks and the lay equivalent—corporate warriors). If you buy one, you really should know roughly what it says, otherwise people will dismiss you as an airhead (like Japanese girls who wear T-shirts inscribed with incomprehensible English, French, or Italian phrases—which they never query but are considered "cute" or, worse, "fashionable").

There are three main hands or scripts: *sōsho* or "running hand" is the most attractive to me, with its graceful curves and pace (but is barely legible to modern Japanese unless trained as calligraphers). The *kaisho* style has very square letters and is thus easier to read, but it is angular and ungraceful, while *gyōsho* lies halfway between. The poems chosen may have no special meaning for you but some knowledge is vital for appreciation, even if this is hard to come by. Calligraphy teachers and scholars are scarce.

However, calligraphy is a widely practiced art. Innumerable exhibitions are held annually with different groups favoring one syllabary, such as *hiragana*, a seasonal theme, or literary topic. From an early age, teachers or parents urge schoolchildren to make their *kakizome* or first calligraphy of the year in early January. Since all *kanji* are expected to fit into the same space, however few or many strokes they have, this provides a lifelong introduction to space, balance, and perspective. I believe learning *kanji* contributes to the lasting interest in cartoons and animation and widespread visual skill. Little four- or five-character Zen statements are most suitable

as starters. Shortly after I came to Japan, a friend gave me a scroll done by her mother. It says *shikai shunpū*, "four seas; a spring wind." Four seas implies all the seas and so the whole world, while a spring wind suggests the benefits of peace and prosperity. This charming scroll endeared her and the country to me. Mieko is still a good friend, so her spring wind has worked wonders.

Visitors to meeting or reception rooms at Japanese companies, or Tea people, will have the opportunity to see many screens and scrolls, some exhorting greater effort and others extolling the Way.

Screen Sizes

Folding screens (*byōbu*) are large, flexible decorative items which were often the central point of aesthetic attraction in a palace, temple, or home. They helped illuminate a room by reflecting light, and served to divide space. For example, the women's quarters could be separated from the men's, the owner's from the servants'. They were also carried by servants to form a windbreak at picnics.

When we read about the history of sixteenth- and seventeenth-century Japan, we are struck by how much attention was paid by the rulers and sub-rulers to having the best painters do the most magnificent screen paintings, thus creating the aura that still surrounds screens. The defenses and imposing lines of their castles were important, but the aesthetic content mattered just as much in winning plaudits from society. This has left an incredible legacy of beautiful pieces by artists in the Kanō line (painters to the court for generations), Tosa studio painters, and many others who did not necessarily sign their work, especially if it was for a grandee, but had learned in the same ateliers.

Fig. 37

Fig. 34 Kanō Tangen, "Flower Cart with Large Wheels," six-panel screen, colors on paper, mid–late 19th c., 5 ft 8 in x 12 ft (1.7 x 3.6 m). Photo courtesy Liza Hyde.

Fig. 35 Kanō Tanshin, "Double Flower Carts," with baskets and various flowers, six-panel screen, gold background, ca. 1800, 5 ft 8 in x 12 ft 5 in (1.7 x 3.8 m). Photo courtesy Liza Hyde.

Fig. 36 Oka Shumboku (1680–1763), "Flower Cart with Children," left-hand of pair of six-panel screens, early 18th c., each 5 ft 9 in x 12 ft 5 in (1.7 x 3.6 m). Photo courtesy Liza Hyde.

Fig. 37 Anon., "Winter Scenes with Birds," left hand of pair of six-panel screens, colors on paper, 18th c., each 5 ft 8 in x 12 ft (1.7m x 3.6 m). Photo courtesy Liza Hyde.

Fig. 38

Artists in China, Korea, and Japan normally produced pairs of six-fold screens. In Japan, these were roughly the height of a man, but some were only 12 inches (30 cm) high and might have only two panels if made to decorate a small space or to hide something. Tea people often used smaller screens in the reduced confines of tea houses and more especially near the corner where tea was made. A wooden frame (often lacquered) was covered with layers of paper and the folds joined together. The painting was done on silk applied to this base. Thin squares of gold and silver foil were often applied round the design to make it look more sumptuous.

This book is aimed at those with the interest and financial capacity to occasionally splurge on nice pieces. Readers should realize that screens worth having for a special place in their home are not likely to be low-priced.

A panel nearly 6 feet (1.8 meters) high and 18 inches (46 cm) wide is already large so that when you think that an artist had twelve panels to fill, painting a pair of screens was clearly a major undertaking and an opportunity to make a statement. Historical masterpieces may be beyond the means of the average collector (many are already in museums), but you can see still wonderful examples at high-class dealers—and then you start saving! The great artists in the genre are mentioned in the chapter on Japan's Art Heritage while the photographs here show some of the wide variety of wonderful pieces still available.

Not all screens are old (some are still made today) and the price differs greatly between works by famous artists (many thousands of dollars) and workshops where very ordinary commercial painting is done (a few zeros); those works are not great art. Indeed, some screens use printed designs, rather like printed wallpaper. These should be cheap, as Japanese prefer not to buy them.

The condition of a screen matters a great deal. If the painting itself is undamaged, then other problems such as holes in the backing paper or a frame that needs repairing or refinishing can be fixed fairly easily in Japan and art centers in London, New York, and Los Angeles, though it does have a cost.

I should advise you never to buy a screen with serious damage to the front (the back matters less since it is usually unseen) as the repair bill will be unjustifiably high, unless the artist is well known or the screen has great artistic or historical value. However, if the individual panels of a screen appeal, then the sky is the limit.

Most Westerners prefer single screens, fortunately, as they are likely to cost less! The purist prefers pairs, especially if they come with a box, as it means they are easier to store, transport, and authenticate. They also appeal for their sense of completeness.

Common is a kind of patchwork screen with attached old scrolls or fans. They can be very attractive. A Swiss neighbor once bought such a screen and a small part was signed Kanō Tanyū, the famous artist (1602–74). Before it was exported, customs officials became agitated about losing a national treasure until an expert assured them it was a fake and the fan dated from the nineteenth century! It was nevertheless very decorative.

Westerners often raise screens, especially smaller ones, by mounting them on legs or placing them flat against the wall on mounts. This allows the screens to be decorations, not furniture, and hence they take up no floor space. They may fit in better with the interior too and experience less wear and tear at the bottom, from being moved around or tripped on.

Fusuma are sliding doors to a Westerner. In this sense, they are not fixed and can be taken out and moved elsewhere at any time. Paintings on them may get rubbed by other doors sliding against them and so their condition can deteriorate badly. They are scarcely painted today, except to replace old doors on temples or shrines. Nice images on silk or paper are often transferred to other media. They are solid, heavy doors and I doubt if they are collectible.

Fig. 38 Anon., "Birds," six-panel screen, mineral colors on paper, 18th c., 20 in x 126 in (50 x 320 cm). Photo courtesy Liza Hyde.

Fig. 39 Anon., "Two Bears amongst Pine Trees and Water," six-panel screen, late 19th c., 5 ft 71/2 in x 12 ft 2 in (1.7 x 3.7 m). Photo courtesy Liza Hyde.

Fig. 40 Kanō School, "Flower Carts," left-hand of pair of six-panel screens, unsigned, ink, color, *gofun*, and gold, 17th c., each 5 ft 6 in x 12 ft 41/2 in (1.7 x 3.8 m), purchased by French diplomat in Japan in 1949. Screens depict *gosho guruma* (courtiers' carriages) laden with seasonal flowers (right: bush clover, hydrangea, dianthus, gentian, freesia, peony, chrysanthemum, morning glory; left: striped bamboo with blue blooms, camellia, chrysanthemum, hibiscus, wisteria, iris, peony, pinks) in porcelain, pottery, bamboo, wicker, and wood vessels. Photo courtesy Liza Hyde.

Fig. 39

Fig. 40

Fig. 41

Fig. 41 Anon., "Emperor Xuan-Zong of T'ang Dynasty" (with favorite consort Yang Gui-fei and ladies-in-waiting divided into two camps, fighting with flowers), six-panel screen, ink and color on paper, 18th c., 6 ft x 12 ft (1.8 x 3.6 m). Photo courtesy Liza Hyde.

Fig. 42

Fig. 43

Hanging Scrolls (Kakejiku or Kakemono)

The fixed frame picture of the West, hung for decades on the same wall, was unknown to the Orient where hanging scrolls (*kakejiku* or *kakemono*) could be rolled up and easily stored away. The designs were painted or drawn on silk or paper laid on paper. At the heavy bottom end were rollers made of ivory, wood, or porcelain. Additional little weights were placed on each end to keep the scroll from moving too much if there was a draft. At the top there were two flaps (*futai*) which hung down and strings from each side going up to the hanging cord. Matching paper and surrounds play a great role in bringing out the qualities of a scroll—not a job for beginners.

Traditional Japanese paintings (*nihonga*) use mineral pigments, unlike the oil-based pigments of the West. This means that they are dreamier and cleaner in a way. They can stand being rolled up and taken out now and then (quite often, in fact), but of course their condition is not improved by it and it should be done with great care. Some scrolls get framed nowadays, as in the West, to prevent damage to the paint or Indian ink, but most scrolls in antiquarian quarters are rolled as in the past and stored in a box, perhaps within another if particularly cherished. There is likely to be an inscription (on the inner or outer) box saying what kind of work it is and by whom, as this saves getting it out each time to check in a store or private storehouse. In cheaper stores, they are hung in rows.

Since about 1600, the most cherished place for a scroll was the *tokonoma*, a ceremonial alcove placed slightly off-center in important rooms. Usually on the left, it is set aside for beauty, not utility, like a mantelpiece in the West. (You might not believe that statement in certain *ryokan* and *minshuku* (inns) where the *tokonoma*

gets stuffed with televisions, telephones, or safes.) The alcove may hold a seasonal flower arrangement and hanging scroll. The important guest will always be seated in front of it, the place of honor.

Scrolls were changed frequently to suit the season, mood, or occasion—to honor a special guest, for example, or to suit the flowers in a room. After the war, when Japanese wages were low, there was a brisk demand from American soldiers for decorative scrolls, mainly of kimonoed women, on strips of silk not made into formal pieces or signed. These were taken home and spread widely. They are still quite cheap and make pleasant gifts but are not exactly art either, as they were mass-produced.

An important distinction is made between paintings on silk (*kempon*) and those on much less expensive and more fragile paper. Remounting silk is feasible so it has a potentially longer life. A work's life is determined by the backing paper and mount, as well as by its treatment. Another drastic gap is between original and printed works—therefore lower-priced, still desirable for those not on six-figure incomes.

Hand Scrolls (E-maki or E-makimono)

Hand scrolls (*e-maki*) are attached to two wooden rollers which you roll in your hands from right to left, as that is how Chinese and Japanese were long written: vertical columns run from right to left. (Nowadays, fiction and literary works such as criticism are usually still written like that, as well as cartoon books, but textbooks and how-to type books read like Western books, from left to right; surprisingly the Chinese have taken to it for everything).

You unroll the left-hand roller as you roll up the right-hand

---

Fig. 42 Anon., "Chrysanthemums," two-panel screen, gold leaf, raised flowers, early 17th c., 6 ft x 5 ft 7 in (1.8 x 1.7 m). Photo courtesy Liza Hyde.

Fig. 43 Rimpa School, "Flowers in Landscape with Fence," two-panel screen, color on paper, early 18th c., 4 ft 5 in x 4 ft 7 in (1.3 x 1.4 m). Photo courtesy Liza Hyde.

Fig. 44 Anon., "Deer," six-panel screen, gold leaf, mineral colors, 18th c., 5 ft 6 in x 8 ft (1.7 x 2.4 m). Photo courtesy Liza Hyde.

Fig. 45 Anon., "Fans and Waves," six-panel screen, color on paper, early 18th c., 5 ft 3 in x 11 ft 8 in (1.6 x 3.6 m). Photo courtesy Liza Hyde.

Fig. 46 Anon., "Hawks with Baby Chicks," six-panel screen, color on paper, 18th c., 54 ft 9$_{1/2}$ in x 9 ft 2 in (16.7 x 2.8 m). Photo courtesy Liza Hyde.

Fig. 44

Fig. 45

Fig. 46

Fig. 47

Fig. 47 Anon., but connected to Imperial family because of jewel-like bronze corners and backing paper with imperial crest in gold, "Emperor's Garden," six-panel screen, *sumi* and colors with gold leaf on paper, early 17th c., 5ft 11 in x 12 ft 6 in (1.8 x 3.8 m). Photo courtesy Liza Hyde.

Fig. 48

Fig. 48 Anon., "Tales of Genji," scenes from five chapters of classic Heian period novel, six-panel screen, ink, color, and gold on paper, 5 ft 7 in x 12 ft 3 1/2 in (1.7 x 3.8 m). Photo courtesy Liza Hyde.

Fig. 52

deserve a serious partner, so should get close to a famous dealer who has an interest in guarding unsullied her/his reputation and so will respect you for asking for the best.

Avoid printed pieces if you are hoping to make money eventually. They will never become expensive: if they did, somebody would print a few thousand more. If you want to decorate a room, they are fine and cheaper than originals and may indeed be by famous artists—originally!

Paper and silk were both used for making scrolls and screens. Paper is cheaper but is less resistant to tearing. The condition of a screen or scroll is absolutely vital because re-backing or extensive restoration can cost major sums of money. A Pittsburgh friend had a two-panel screen done up in Japan for $700. Before leaving the country, he realized that taking it back to the US would cost too much and he had the screen auctioned. He received just a third of the cost of the remounting alone.

A screen or scroll should have no obvious damage or dirty marks. The condition of the paper on the back is not so important, as changing that is not dear and can be done later. Besides, guests will not normally see it. People who love paper will find that scrolls are backed by a fantastic array of different papers.

Washi has an unrivalled place in the paper world, being strong and of infinite variety. (See Sukey Hughes' comprehensive book on the subject.) I have bought several cheap scrolls for the paper alone! Though less paper is made by hand these days, there are still villages like Kurodani or Najio which depend on it for their livelihood.

Fig. 53

Fig. 54

Fig. 52 "Amida Coming over the Mountain," hanging scroll, color on silk, 13th c., 4 ft x 2 ft 6 in (1.2 x 0.7 m). National Treasure, Kyoto National Museum. Unusually, Amida looks half to the left, right hand up, left hand down. Photo courtesy Kyoto National Museum.

Fig. 53 Itō Jakuchū (1716–1800), "Cocks and Hens," *fusuma* painting, 1790, detail from set of nine wall panels formerly in Kai-hō-ji, Fushimi, Kyoto. Photo courtesy Kyoto National Museum.

Fig. 54 "Crows on a Plum Branch" (detail), six door panels attributed to Unkoku Tōgan (1547–1618), colors and gold leaf on paper, each 5 ft 4 in x 5 ft 1 in (1.6 x 1.5 m). Panels originally at

Najima Castle (built 1588–9). Typical Momoyama composition of huge plum with crows in the snow. Photo courtesy Kyoto National Museum.

Fig. 55

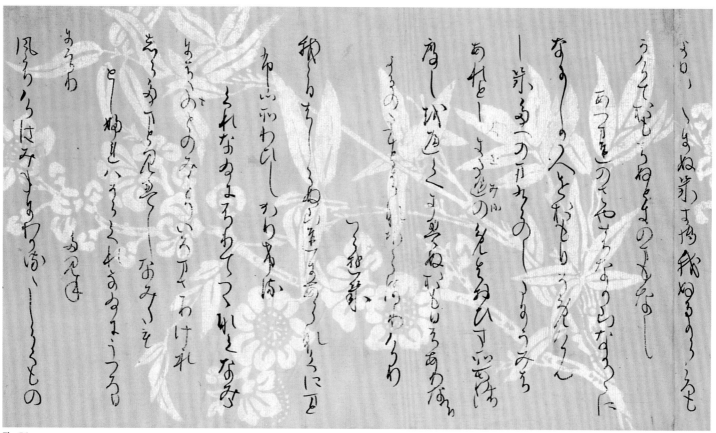

Fig. 56

Choosing Screens and Scrolls

Choosing furniture has certain practical aspects, such as do the drawers hold enough or will it fit into a particular space? Non-utilitarian art objects require different criteria.

First impressions are important. As dealer Sōbian of Kyoto says, "Does it hit you in the eyes?" The movement of the paint brush (*e-suji*) is important. For example, the *susuki* (eulalia or pampas grass) should not look flaccid but stand erect. Jot down the artist's name, period, and condition, and if it is an original piece or a print, or if it has been repaired. "The name may not matter to you now, but it is vital for possible resale—and for chatting to guests."

Think how the screen or scroll will go with the color of your sofa or with the curtains. In Japan, a conscientious dealer may take a screen or scroll to a client's house if he is strongly interested. Some dealers do not like to do this, as it is time-consuming and may cause wear and tear. Also ask about "after care."

The air-conditioning of some Westerners' houses is direct and may tear screens or stain scrolls. Insist that the seller be willing to help with little repairs later if affected by air-conditioning.

Many Westerners like *kachō* (still lifes of flowers and birds). Those who tire of them, purchase simple designs of the moon or sun. *Karako* (Chinese boys) are not popular among Westerners (too cute perhaps?). Lawyers seem to like hawks and tigers, as their strong or fierce looks suggest winning lawsuits, says Sōbian.

Galleries in capitals tend to be more expensive than elsewhere but inevitably they have better works and the dealers provide much more information; if they do, purchasing there is a good bet.

A sense of season permeates the designs on hanging scrolls, but less so screens. When you first buy a scroll, you should purchase a work you like, without worrying about its season. Few are devoid of season. Flowers are inevitably seasonal. If you buy several hanging scrolls, you may develop a sense of season. If you do, you should think carefully about the seasonal element when making later purchases. But don't be a toady. Become an Antipodean!

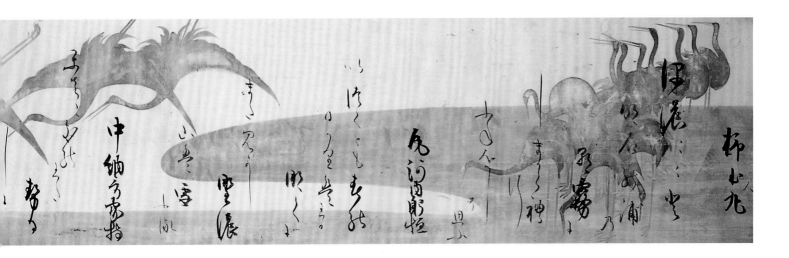

Fig. 57

Fig. 55 Crane designs, lower detail from collection of calligraphy by Hon'ami Kōetsu and painting by Tawaraya Sōtatsu, hand scroll, ink and paper, 17th c., 1 ft 11 in x 44 ft 5 in (58 cm x 13.6 m), extraordinary elegance. Photo courtesy Kyoto National Museum.

Fig. 56 *Kokin Wakashū* (love poem) calligraphy, hand scroll, ink on decorated paper, 11th c., 6 1/2 in x 8 ft (16 cm x 2.4 m), attributed to Ono no Tōfū (894–966), the great calligrapher, but

in the collection of Hon'ami, Kyoto National Museum. Most celebrated *meibutsu-gire* (famous fragment). Photo courtesy Kyoto National Museum.

Fig. 57 Hokusai (1760–1849), "Shell Gathering," hanging scroll, color on silk, early 19th c., 1 ft 8 in x 2 ft 8 in (50 x 81 cm). Photo courtesy Osaka Municipal Museum of Art.

Genuineness

It would take a few volumes to describe what could happen with art. Here I shall mention a few precautions, starting with "use your head" and "use your eyes." Look at the ends and back of the scroll or screen you are considering buying. If the dealer says a piece is very old and there is no evidence of wear, something is amiss. If a scroll has been kept very carefully in a box within a box and only taken out once a year, it may look almost new, but consider if it is likely that you can buy such a treasure if low-priced—it belonged to a rich man or connoisseur. If the amount of visible wear agrees with the age mentioned by the dealer, then things look better.

A screen stands on the ground and gets pushed open and shut,

Fig. 58

Fig. 59

Fig. 58 Kansai Mori Koshuku (1814–94), figure, probably Yang Gui-fei, mistress of Emperor Ming Huang, late autumn, hanging scroll, 1871, 7 ft 4 in x 2 ft 8 in (2.2 m x 81 cm). Photo courtesy Liza Hyde.

Fig. 59 Sakai Dōitsu, "Yūgao" (bottle gourds), hanging scroll, silk on paper, 1870–90, 5 ft 5 in x 1 ft 5 in (1.7 m x 43 cm). Sakai Dōitsu was a pupil of the famous Sakai Hōitsu of the Rimpa School. Both were good at *kachō* (flowers and birds). Rimpa painters liked the *tarashikomi* technique used here where another pigment is added while the previous pigment is not yet dry, so that colors run and generate unique colors. Photo courtesy Gallery Sōbian.

Fig. 60 Mio Goseki, "Tora" (tiger), hanging scroll, Meiji era, 6 ft 9 in x 1 ft 9 in (2.1 m x 53 cm). Mio Goseki was a pupil of Ōhashi Suiseki. Both excelled at tiger pictures. Photo courtesy Gallery Sōbian.

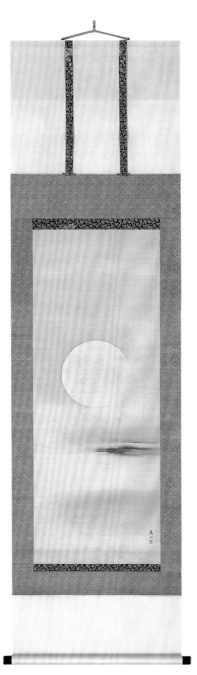

Fig. 60

Fig. 61

Fig. 62

or to change its shape. This friction should be visible, even if the base of the screen is protected by metal plates on the corners. No wear, no age. In fact, age is not necessary. A new screen can be very nice and easier to fit into Western surroundings, but if the seller insists that it is old and unrepaired, then something is wrong and you may not trust him/her.

Traditionally, screens and scrolls were boxed. If that box is a *tomobako*, or accompanying box, there may well be a name, date and signature. If these details do not match those on the work, the work should sell for less than otherwise. The signature on some

works has been added later and this completely changes society's valuation. English readers are unlikely to ever get to the stage of really knowing signatures, but they can look at materials and check that they look right.

Screens and scrolls fit into Western rooms only after thought. They are a diadem of Japanese civilization and often examples of great art, so it is worth thinking creatively. If you buy what an expert or two also think has aesthetic value and is in good condition, then it will become a family heirloom, not an Enron or WorldCom. stock certificate.

Fig. 61 Uchida Gozan, "Chūshū get-surin" (harvest moon), hanging scroll, Meiji era, 6 ft 6 in x 1 ft 8 in (2 m x 51 cm). The design is interesting as the moon is depicted by delicate light and dark areas of *sumi*. Photo courtesy Gallery Sōbian.

Fig. 62 Takenaka Kidō, "Hotaru" (fire-flies) and summer grasses, hanging scroll, Meiji era, 6 ft 4 in x 1 ft 8 in (1.9 m x 51 cm). Kidō is not so famous

but fireflies are popular because their lifetime is so short: a picture of them captures a moment. Photo courtesy Gallery Sōbian.

(Overleaf) Fig. 63 *Ema* (horse votive tablet), commemorative funeral paint-ing on wood, 2 ft 9 in x 4 ft 8 1/2 in (84 cm x 1.4 m). Photo courtesy Liza Hyde.

Fig. 63

浮世絵 版画

UKIYO-E AND OTHER PRINTS

The earliest prints to be made in Japan were ordered by the Empress in 664. Although a lot of early prints are repetitive, the better ones have fine color and line and are Buddhist in origin and theme. The techniques were brought from China. One acquired merit by regularly drawing, painting, or printing as many Buddhist images as possible, so educated devotees and priests produced a great number. This practice weakened with declining religious fervor from the fourteenth century. Since they were both cheap and portable, prints then became souvenirs of temples and shrines for visiting pilgrims.

Some people collect these prints, but the main collecting channels are described in the next sections. However, an interesting collection of old Buddhist prints was described by Meher McArthur in *Daruma* 16. Such prints are mainly sought by scholars or those deeply interested in religion, as their focus is on parts of religious life foreign to us.

Fig. 65

Woodblock Prints (Ukiyo-e)

Woodblocks were long used to publish books with or without images, but *ukiyo-e* pictures of the Floating (or entertainment/ pleasure) World started from around 1665 when Japan finally enjoyed peace and rising prosperity. With money but little freedom, townsmen devoted themselves to pleasure: time was often spent drinking or at brothels and kabuki theaters.

People wore fancy clothes and enjoyed extravagant lifestyles and to express themselves sought an art form unlike those of the court or Buddhist monks. *Ukiyo-e* thus celebrated a hedonistic society. Sensual courtesans in the most popular and stylish costumes, and dramatic scenes from kabuki plays were the main subjects. The works did not moralize like priests, nor depict an aesthetically ideal landscape like court painters.

Initially, the subject matter of *ukiyo-e* was up-market, with masked references to Chinese literature or *Genji Monogatari* episodes. After about 1800, however, woodblock prints no longer appealed only to this leisured, educated class, but to ordinary people with everyday interests. Nowadays, those same people would focus on television or movies, but the kabuki theater then was where the heart-throbs were. Many woodblock prints show an actor in a favorite, climactic pose (*mie*) and were bought by his fans as they were cheap and attractive mementos.

All over the land a main reason for buying prints made in Tokyo was to see the latest fashions worn by actors and courtesans. In this sense, prints foreran fashion magazines and television. With the regular, enforced sojourns by clansmen in the capital, many prints got taken home to the clan lands, so men and women could see the latest clothes and hairstyles prevailing in the capital.

Top fashion photographs are snapped by the very best today but with Edo prints, there was a difference. The best-connected aspiring artists got into famous Kanō and Tosa school studios and could expect a secure career, but the *ukiyo-e* world was treated by the samurai class with disdain: those without the right connections had to risk the nether world of *ukiyo-e*, because that was where the

---

(Previous page) Fig. 64 Hiroshige (1797–1858), "100 Views of Famous Places in Edo—Kawaguchi no Watashi Zenkōji," woodblock print, 1857. Photo courtesy Mita Arts Gallery.

Note: Ukiyo-e were made before concepts of limited editions existed; artists' birth and death dates may be uncertain. Standard sizes include *Ōban*: 15 x 10 in (38 x 25 cm), but sometimes half an inch smaller; *Chūban*: 8 x 11 in (20 x 28 cm), and *Hosoban*: 6 x 12 in (15 x 30 cm).

Fig. 65 Masanobu (1686–1764), "Man and Three Ladies," woodblock print, *sumizuri-e* (black and white print), ca. 1715. Photo courtesy Mita Arts Gallery.

Fig. 66 Toyoharu (1735–1814), "Elegance: Six Clear Rivers," woodblock print. Photo courtesy Mita Arts Gallery.

Fig. 67 Kiyonaga (1752–1815), "Minami Jūnikō," woodblock print, ca. 1785. Photo courtesy Mita Arts Gallery.

Fig. 68 Koryūsai (fl. late 18th c.), *chūban*, woodblock print, ca. 1770. Photo courtesy Mita Arts Gallery.

Fig. 66

Fig. 67

Fig. 68

Fig. 69

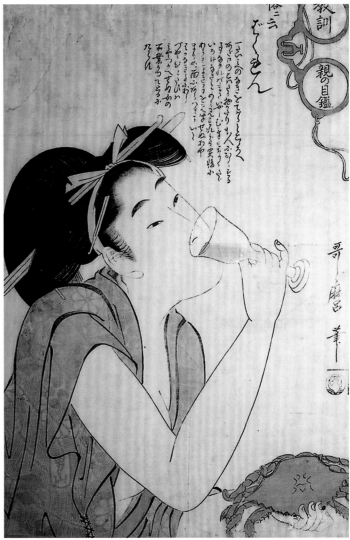

Fig. 70

work was and fame might come among the townspeople (but maybe not money). Colleague Peter Ujlaki says that apart from Hokusai (who did get painting and *surimono* or print commissions, but was careless with money like the typical *Edokko* so always out of pocket), artists accepted lower prestige to work in *ukiyo-e*, generally out of a love for the lifestyle of the theater and amusement districts, so they worked for love not lucre.

A third, if less common, reason for the existence of prints was to advertise a particular establishment or kimono design. The Floating World, epitomized by Yoshiwara in Edo, was very competitive, and since some prints bear the names of geisha houses, it is reasonable to see a connection. Many prints of women name their place of work. Thus, prints would have been a good way to show which lovely women worked where and what they wore.

Occasionally, a woman might give a regular client a print of herself as a token of affection or to remind him where to find her—in much the same way that name cards are used today! Some experts, however, do not share this reasoning.

Judging by the current passion for erotic prints and animation, another merit of prints must have been that they fed the Japanese people's insatiable appetite for the visual. As a northern European, in the wrong mood I find the visual clutter of Japan (and Hong Kong, etc.) an eyesore, but there is also something charming about a narrow street full of vertical signs—ergo these prints.

It is interesting to note that Japanese cartoons and fashions are increasingly popular in other Asian countries.

Popularity in the West

Westerners have always felt the pull of *ukiyo-e*, probably because they show landscapes, clothing, and a way of life quite unlike anything in Europe or America. As a result, many dealers, curators, and collectors have considerable knowledge of the subject, while museums, auction houses, and stores are well stocked with prints.

Woodblock images of the Floating World became popular from the 1860s in the West, captivating people with their vitality, freshness, and charm, and causing the Japonisme art movement. *Ukiyo-e* were collected by Van Gogh, Gauguin, and Monet. In a way, Westerners are responsible for rescuing *ukiyo-e* from oblivion, as most indigenous critics scorned them in the later 1800s, though aware that the print artist Utamaro was different and that Westerners loved Hokusai and Hiroshige too.

Ukiyo-e influence is seen in masters like Van Gogh, Whistler, and Toulouse-Lautrec, dating from the time when *ukiyo-e* by unknowns were said at times to be but liner in a box of curios packed for European travelers, or sold by the pound to curio collectors, sometimes after being dirtied to make them appear "older."

One secret of the enduring popularity of *ukiyo-e* is the way some artists went beyond the Japanese tradition of using line and sensitivity to convey scenes, and incorporated perspective (putting Westerners at ease) in scenes that are still quintessentially exotic, thereby inducing *frissons* of both recognition and shock. Other reasons are the soaring creative imagination shown in choosing

Fig. 71

Fig. 69 Utamaro, "Three Beauties," one of triptych, ca. 1800. Photo courtesy Mita Arts Gallery.

Fig. 70 Utamaro, "Teachings in Parents' Eyes—Bakuren" (abandoned woman), woodblock print, ca. 1802. Photo courtesy Mita Arts Gallery.

Fig. 71 Toyokuni I (1769–1825), "Today's Match of Beauties—Saké Cup as Mirror," woodblock print, ca. 1820. Photo courtesy Mita Arts Gallery.

Fig. 72 Toyokuni I, "Fireworks at Ryō-goku," woodblock print, triptych, ca. 1790. Photo courtesy Mita Arts Gallery.

Fig. 72

Fig. 73

scenery (see later, Hokusai and Hiroshige), the human warmth of genre scenes like the inebriated revelers and snoozing dogs in Kuniyoshi's "Yoshiwara Embankment by Moonlight," and the playfulness of Hiroshige's "Ratcatcher" or Kuniyoshi's "Six Immortal Poets as Cats," which satirizes the Chinese tradition of making respectful images of famous authors. Through punning allusions to them or their poems, it depicts six fat cats socializing: the great Heian era poets (*Rokkasen*) Ariwara no Narihira, Ono no Komachi (the lasting image of female beauty and poetic excellence), Sōjō Henjō, Bunya no Yasuhide, Kisen Hōshi, and Ōtomo no Kuronushi.

Lastly, *ukiyo-e* and literature had close connections. Many artists studied poetry, like haiku, *waka* (five-line poems), and *kyōka* (satirical poems) and added them to prints. This literary dimension adds to our appreciation of their images, if explained.

To fully understand *ukiyo-e*, one should know the lineage of the various schools and who studied under whom. For brevity, this book leaves the reader to go to other sources for that information and this chapter provides just an overview.

A tradition emerged a hundred years ago of writing off most artists working after the early nineteenth century. Some artists then, and earlier, lacked originality but many prints of the first half of the nineteenth century display superb draftsmanship, conception, and execution. *Fin de siècle* disapproval had other currents and reasons, but lingers. Collectors should use their own eyes to find out what is good, not rely on Victorian prejudice; then some thought Hiroshige was the last great artist. Recent books on prolific Kunisada, bloodthirsty Yoshitoshi, and Kiyochika (who immortalized scenes from the Sino-Japanese and Russo-Japanese Wars of 1894–5 and 1904–5) show how much longer the genre survived—with greatness!

Creativity of Erotic Prints (Shunga)

One area of *ukiyo-e* long kept hidden was the enormous output of erotic prints (a third or more of the total *ukiyo-e* output, according to some estimates). Called *shunga*, they traditionally showed men and women with enormous sexual organs cavorting with glee, sometimes eyed by similarly active humans, mice, or dogs in the background. These pictures embarrassed the modernizers of the Meiji era and influenced several generations of Japanese into instant disapproval, for social or religious reasons, despite the long tradition of erotic art in the country (just as mixed bathing was later banned) after Western, especially missionary, criticism.

They still offend traditional family types and often governments, but the genre is fascinating as art (the prints often display impeccable draftsmanship), as social history (the boudoir and traditional furnishings are lavishly displayed), and as a facet of a way of life that is no more.

Even in recent years, astonishingly amusing works have been created. I have a recent hand scroll of dubious intent but great amusement value in which all the actors show appropriate *sang-froid*. Among others, it depicts men with immense members engaged in "member wrestling"; the shaved pate of a kowtowing samurai is shown to closely resemble a nearby circumcised member head; a kimonoed male dancer performs on a tightrope supported by two giant erect members; like snake charmers, a *shamisen* (three-string ukulele) and a flute player encourage a top to continue spinning on another erection, amid many other tricks of imaginative fantasy.

In 1995, the Japanese government finally loosened the

Fig. 98

Fig. 99

Fig. 97 Charles Bartlett (1860–1940), "Kobe," woodblock print, 1916, 15 x 10 in (38 x 25 cm). Photo courtesy Mita Arts Gallery.

Fig. 98 Oda Kazuma (1882–1956), "Night in Utsunomiya," woodblock print, 1928. Photo courtesy Mita Arts Gallery.

Fig. 99 Kawase Hasui (1883–1957), "Waves of Echigo Bay," woodblock print, 1921. Photo courtesy Mita Arts Gallery.

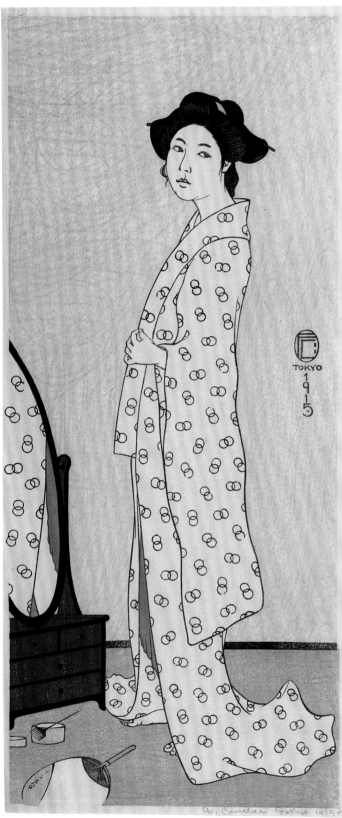

Fig. 101

Fig. 100

Fig. 102

Fig. 100 Fritz Capelari (1884–1950), "Woman Standing Before a Mirror," woodblock print, 1915, 16 x 7 in (41 x 18 cm). Photo courtesy Mita Arts Gallery.

Fig. 101 Ohara Koson (1877–1945), "Peacocks on Pine Trees," woodblock print, ca. 1925. Photo courtesy Mita Arts Gallery.

Fig. 102 Akamatsu Rinsaku (1878–1953), "Kobe Wharf, 1917," from the series "Hanshin Meisho Zue," a transitional series before the full blossoming of *shin hanga*. Foreigners arrive with a nanny and pet bird. Photo courtesy Peter Ujlaki.

(Opposite) Fig. 103 Yamamura Kōka (1885–1942), "Dancing Scene at the New Carlton in Shanghai," woodblock print, 1925. Photo courtesy Mita Arts Gallery.

Fig. 104

Fig. 105

Early Historical Records

Like many old things in Japan, *sagemono* have been little documented. Most were in use by the end of the sixteenth century, while the brush holder and *inrō* probably date earlier, from the twelfth and fourteenth centuries respectively. The earliest extant and datable *sagemono* was found in the 1636 tomb of Date Masamune (lord of Sendai), so the *sagemono* was made before that. According to Arakawa Hirokazu, former head curator of the Tokyo National Museum, the *Mezamashigusa* colophon of 1625 clearly refers to "a hanging *inrō* with *nashiji* decoration."

He notes too that the 1686 *Yōshūfushi* gazette "lists *inrō* as one of the craft products of Kyoto, indicating that there was widespread demand for them and suggesting perhaps that they were produced by specialists." He adds, "The *Jinrin Kinmo zui* (1690) records that *inrōshi* (*inrō* makers) were to be found in several different places and illustrates a lacquer-decorated *inrō*."

Our first detailed source is *Sōken Kishō*, published in 1781 by an Osaka sword dealer, Inaba Michitatsu (also read Tsūryū). It listed fifty-seven famous *netsuke* carvers and thirty-seven *inrō* makers then living (adding that there had to be hundreds more). It divided the *netsukeshi* (*netsuke* carvers) into schools based on geography; so there was an understanding even then that this was work of high quality. The book lists nineteen *inrōshi* in Edo, seven in Kyoto, six in Kanazawa, and three in Osaka, whereas this city had by far the most *netsukeshi*. Unfortunately, this was the only book to appear until Westerners started collecting and writing in the late nineteenth century, so our knowledge of earlier times is limited.

Ueda Reikichi, the first modern Japanese *sagemono* theorist, suggested in *The Netsuke Handbook*, that the Japanese have been blessed with nimble fingers and their crafts are characterized by exceptional delicacy, precision, and exquisiteness. In his opinion, *netsuke* were an excellent example of the craftsman's natural gifts as they were made by free people in the sense that they were not working to the orders of a patron (unlike many painters, for example), so had to please only themselves or ordinary customers. Robert Fleischel of Sagemonoya counters that many danglers were commissioned, for example by *daimyō*, so freer but exceptions!

Considerable knowledge of mythology and Japanese literature was a must for artists and clients—and for collectors now. This gives the pieces a depth that adds to the pleasure we feel in owning or admiring them—and sometimes a thrill of discovery.

Fig. 123

Typical Japanese Subjects

As miniature sculptures, *obi* danglers may depict anything, but the subjects tend to fall into particular groups, such as animals, historical figures, and masks, which may break down into more specific subgroups. (Much of the information in the following section applies to all other Japanese arts.)

Zodiac Animals

Orientals pattern the years into cycles of twelve represented by the animals of the Zodiac—the rat, ox, tiger, hare, dragon, snake, horse, goat, monkey, cock, dog, and wild boar—who rushed to Buddha's side on hearing he was dying (but not, of course, the cat which lingered in its own sweet way). These, in turn, come in five more cycles (wood, fire, earth, metal, and water), making a sexagesimal system. Living through five cycles of twelve years is equivalent to the biblical "three score years and ten" for man's life span. Reaching sixty (*kanreki*) merits a big party and dressing in baby red.

Fig. 124

the Bodhisattva Fugen, or a demon laughingly acting as a priest chanting his prayers and fingering a rosary (Fig. 188). Another side of *mitate* is the intellectual linking of current events with the past. Framing something in the distant past that was relevant to today and an implicit criticism—and would be understood by those in the know—was one way of avoiding trouble with the government.

Many well-made *sagemono* have lasted for centuries despite fires, earthquakes, and misuse. Cheap danglers were also made from inferior materials but they would have worn out naturally due to daily bumps and friction. Most of the items collected today were made by artists with superb materials: ivory, lacquer, gold, silver, coral, precious inlays, Indian textiles, cherry, persimmon, ebony and boxwood, amber, horn, and crystal.

The pride that artists/owners felt in their work is visible in these valuable materials and in the large number of signatures on *sagemono* (sometimes two on lacquer and metal *inrō*). Artists might not sign pieces commissioned by *daimyō* or the shōgun (whose status was so much higher), so the lack of one is by no means proof of inferiority. Signatures (for example, that of Tomotada) were often added later and may cause doubts about dating and authenticity. Willi Bosshard noted wholesale falsification in Kyoto ca. 1970.

Netsuke

Netsuke were little toggles connected by a cord through small holes in *sagemono* to counterbalance them. The *netsuke* stayed above the *obi* while the cord slipped down inside and behind it, to hold in place an *inrō* or pouch below. The earliest *sagemono* appear on Kamakura era (1185–1333) hand scrolls but this was probably a fad only for the court. Yet it spread, and we can say that common use of *netsuke* and *inrō* dates back at least four centuries. At first, they were rather simple items but soon they became more and more decorative and refined.

The golden era of *sagemono* was the eighteenth and nineteenth centuries. *Netsuke* were not cheap: Sekido Kengo (*Netsuke Kenkyū Bulletin*, 25) says that in the eighteenth century one particular *netsuke* sold for the price of a house! Ivory was always dear.

The promotion of Western dress (with its trouser pockets) rang the knell of *sagemono*, as there was no longer any need for an *obi* from which to hang things. *Netsuke* were discarded by the tens of thousands between 1870 and 1900 and were often bought by Westerners. Thus a great many went overseas to form the basis of museum collections and scholarship. *Netsukeshi* started making less refined works for tourists. Some continued the good old ways for the remaining connoisseurs and collectors at home and abroad, or developed new directions like the Sō school.

Fig. 132

Fig. 133

The International Netsuke Society has some 600 members, with chapters in the US, Europe, and Japan. Lectures are given and new members learn the intricacies of these fascinating little toggles. For years the purists who say that only old *netsuke* are real have skirmished with those who collect *netsuke* for their beauty and so support some of the very skillful modern *netsukeshi* in Australia, Europe, Japan, and the US. One controversial piece, by Clive Hallam, shows a snail on a Coca Cola can (poor snail—will it survive the citric and phosphoric acids?), thus modernizing the traditional motif of a snail on a well bucket (Fig. 135).

Netsuke range from 1 inch (2 cm) to 4 inches (10 cm) in length, although they occasionally reached 6 inches (15 cm) in the eighteenth century. They are primarily made of ivory or wood, especially boxwood, but also of stag antler, marine ivory (like narwhal horn), corozo nuts, seashells, glass, and a number of other substances. They have two little holes (*himotōshi*) in the back or elsewhere if the carver can so arrange the design so that cord can tie the toggle to the *inrō* and *ojime*. This last widget moves up and down the cord to hold closed or open purses, tobacco pouches, and *inrō*.

Fig. 134

Fig. 131a, b *Netsuke* cabinet (opened below), signed Shibayama, and seal, signed Masayoshi (12 x 9 1/2 x 8 in (30 x 24 x 20 cm). Photo courtesy Sagemonoya.

Fig. 132 *Netsuke*, ivory, of demon (*oni*) with large pincers, signed Basetsu Sanjin, 19th c., 2 in (5 cm). Photo courtesy Sagemonoya.

Fig. 133 *Netsuke*, ivory, of ox, signed Tomotada, 18th c., 2 1/4 in (6 cm). Photo courtesy Sagemonoya.

Fig. 134 *Netsuke*, lacquer, of dog, signed Zeshin, late 19th c., 1 1/4 in (3 cm). Photo courtesy Sagemonoya.

Fig. 135

Fig. 136

Another requirement is a smooth exterior: the *netsuke* brushed against the wearer's clothes, so jagged points would catch. Earlier, and sometimes later, one *himotōshi* hole was larger than the other; the knot on the cord could not fit through the smaller one, so was anchored. *Netsuke* were carved all over Japan but tend to fall into different schools, with distinctive materials. In the cities, men had more money and preferred ivory; elsewhere wood was commoner.

Forms of Netsuke

Most *netsuke* were short and compact although variations included a thin, elongated type known as *sashi netsuke*, which was tucked into the *obi* instead of hanging above it, and *obihasami netsuke*, which clipped onto the top and bottom of an *obi*. Other kinds of *netsuke* included masks (Fig. 123), *ryūsa* (pierced, often round *netsuke* named after the inventor) (Fig. 180), and *manjū* (round, bun-like *netsuke*). According to Lawrence Smith, the earliest specially made *netsuke* were flattish disks, now called *manjū netsuke*; and *kagamibuta*, which were round, often with a metal lid (Fig. 181).

Quite a few *netsuke* are termed *shunga netsuke*, which means they are erotic, but in ways that may or may not be obvious. For example, a lid decorated with a mask may be taken off a box to reveal a naked couple; a female Daruma may sound cute but was linked with the tradition of the great Zen teacher experiencing "seven falls but eight arisings," in turn recalling that a whore often went down but also got up; a woman may lick sticky *tororo* grated yam juice—which has sexual connotations. A simple, longer, rounded sculpture may have been designed to suggest alternative uses. Sometimes prurience or the desire to amuse were the aim, but often a desire for children and the happiness they bring was decisive, or the pleasure of wearing something that might catch people's eyes, like a loud tie, deep *décolleté*, or Prada logo.

Netsuke Schools and Artists

In 1600, Osaka was the biggest city in Japan (and the world?), but gradually was overtaken by Edo, the warrior capital, which attracted businessmen and artisans from all over the country. Yet even in 1781, the *Sōken Kishō* records many *netsuke* carvers as being from Osaka. Yoshimura Shūzan, said to be the most famous, never signed his work, so we cannot appraise it. Other artists mentioned are Tsuji, Garaku, Insai, Sankō, Higo, Kajun, and Sōshichi, and several who presumably did not sign their *netsuke* as none have been found. Later Osaka artists include Hidemasa, Shigemasa, and Kaigyokusai

Fig. 137

Fig. 189

Writing Brush Holders (Yatate)

For the warpath, samurai carried an inkstone, inkstick, and brush in their quiver (*yatate*, literally "arrow stand"). In the twelfth to thirteenth century, a new *yatake* was invented—keeping the old name—with a brush in a tube and ink stored in an inkpot. A lid held the brush in and kept the wadding-soaked ink from leaking. There might be a knife for cutting paper or shaping bristles. *Yatate* were usually metal (also wood and bamboo) and poked into an *obi*.

However, that covers only the unibody type. Robert Fleischel in *Daruma* 3 notes the old fan type, seen in Kamakura era scrolls and inspired by a soldier's *tessen* (iron fan, and weapon), as well as *inrō*, both separate and box types. The first two have ink in a separate pot; this dual body type may have areas for seals and knives, while the box type is a smaller ordinary writing box (*suzuri-bako*). Perhaps the most impressive are those in the shape of a gun: some actually fire bullets—effective for frightening, but inaccurate!

Famous smiths like Baitetsu, Tansai, Ryū'undō, and Ryūmondō made *yatate* but also men known for making other *sagemono*. Fleischel mentions, for example, Kokusai, Minkō, Masanao, Shibayama, Hashi'ichi, Rantei, Mitsuhiro, Zeshin, and Kenzan. Over a hundred signatures must remain: this literacy symbol was favored from shōgun to farmer.

Fig. 190

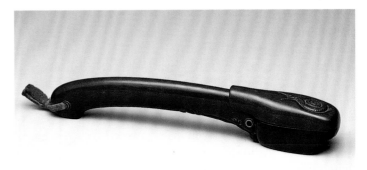

Fig. 191

---

pictures), boxwood with ivory, deer antler, and shellfish inlays, anon., early 19th c., 4 in (10 cm). Photo courtesy Sagemonoya.

Fig. 189 Tobacco pouch, *kinkarakawa* (dressed leather with gold paint and various designs), with gold carp clasp, anon., 19th c., 5 in (13 cm). Photo courtesy Sagemonoya.

Fig. 190 *Yatate*, stag antler, with tiger on lid of inkpot, anon, 19th c., 7³/4 in (20 cm). Photo courtesy Sagemonoya.

Fig. 191 *Yatate*, wood, with design of snail and lizard, anon., 19th c., 7³/4 in (20 cm). Photo courtesy Sagemonoya.

Fig. 192

Fig. 193

Fig. 194

Dummy Swords (Bokutō)

During the Edo period, samurai carried a long and a short sword, but ordinary people wore neither. Since Japan had its fair share of night-time baddies, self-defense was a problem for people out in the dark. This gave rise to the *bokutō*, or "seeming-sword." Its job was to look like a weapon and be workman-like, if applied to an opponent. (Another way of naming it might be "nightstick".)

The normal material for a dummy sword was solid wood. Bladeless, it was curved like a sword but, as happened with many Japanese things, the simple weapon soon grew all kinds of pretty little extras so that they were lacquered, inscribed, or inlaid with various materials and sometimes signed with names famous in the *netsuke* world. Some are full sword length, 26–30 inches (66–76 cm)

but with time they became shorter and more delicate.

Bokutō are rather rare, though they were used during samurai rule from the seventeenth to the nineteenth centuries; probably they were discarded when safety was no longer an issue.

Until recently, the word *bokutō* was translated as "doctor's sword," on the grounds that doctors had to attend patients at night and needed a weapon—and probably a smooth-talking salesman's spiel! However, it is now known that doctors were of sufficiently high status to carry at least one sword and there is no proof that they carried wooden swords anyway. It was a nice theory.

I have a long wooden *yatate* which is close enough to the shape and length of a *bokutō* (it also has the same skull-jangling ability), so it is probable that there was a generally felt need in the country for protection at night.

Fig. 192 *Yatate* (writing brush holder), bamboo, carved in *sukashi-bori*, with matching inkpot, anon, 19th c., 8 1/4 in (21 cm). Photo courtesy Sagemonoya.

Fig. 193 *Yatate*, with lacquered landscape design on ink holder, signed Chikuzan, Meiji era, 9 1/2 in (24 cm). Photo courtesy Sagemonoya.

Fig. 194 *Yatate*, wood, carved in shape of seahorse, with lids opening to show seal pad and inkpot, anon, 19th c., 8 3/4 in (22 cm). Photo courtesy Sagemonoya.

Fig. 195 Four *bokutō* ("seeming-swords"). Top: Inlaid design of plum blossoms, anon, 19th c., 17 1/2 in (44 cm). Second: Lacquer design of plants and insects, anon., 19th c., 17 in (43 cm).

Third: Inlaid design of skull and rosary, anon., 19th c., 18 in (46 cm). Fourth: Design of skull and pine branch, signed Minkō, 19th c., 16 3/4 in (42 cm). Photo courtesy Sagemonoya.

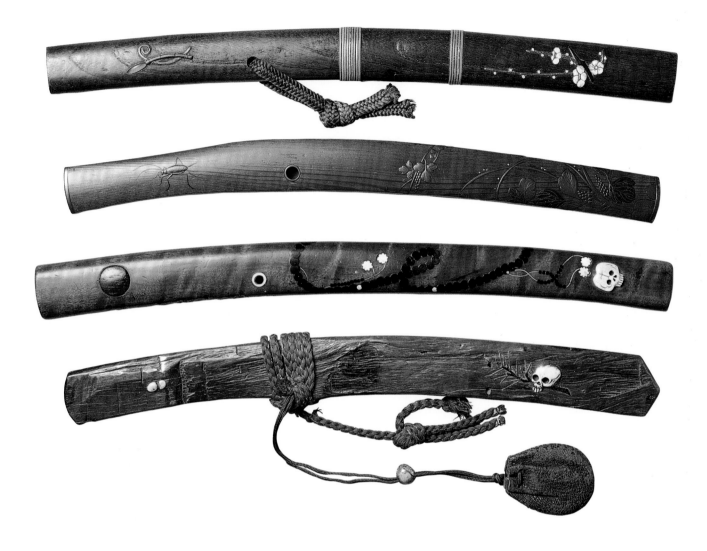

Fig. 195

Miscellaneous

Sagemono means "anything hanging from the waist" so we may add things like the occasional saké flask, or the highly patinated antler tip which would make an ideal gouger or pick, and indeed the gunpowder horn with cicada flap on my shelf, though they are not normally part of the canon.

Occasionally, you are lucky enough to find cabinets for storing *netsuke*. The Tokyo National Museum was given one and another Shibayama beauty is in Fig. 131a, b.

Collecting Sagemono

Top *netsuke* by artists like Masanao of Kyoto and Kaigyokusai can fetch tens of thousands of dollars; the highest price *netsuke* I have heard listed was $240,000 (at the Boston Netsuke Convention, just before September 11th, 2001), though Richard Silverman mentioned $300,000 at the 2004 International Netsuke Society Convention in Honolulu. The prices of quality *inrō* are high, too. Other *sagemono* cost much less as a rule, but if an unprecedented piece perhaps with a famous signature came along, who knows?

Old but commoner shapes and less attractive or damaged pieces may be found for between $100 and US$500. Collector Willi

Bosshard (*Daruma* 39) has come across fake old *netsuke*, even some made in Germany, so care is needed. Long ago he bought one with a fake famous signature but liked the work so much he later asked the Kyoto *netsukeshi* to affix his real name, not that requested by the store: but that cost more than the original purchase!

New *netsuke* made in greater China may cost $50–100 (my record low is $10 and $30 for a new *inrō*, simply because the seller knows a factory). They have similar motifs and materials (fake or composite ivory, or lathe-cut wood) so budget buyers can afford them, but those with more experience want to tap into the feeling of a work being handled over time—especially the smooth patina which marks long use. Most collectors value the genuine over the imitation and also know that, with luck, people will still find *sagemono* desirable in years to come, so the chances are you will not lose money over the decades.

A stray meeting with a cheap *netsuke* can lead the reader on to vertiginous delights of discovery, so I would encourage you to get your hand in with cheap pieces, study them, read specialist books, and walk round galleries and museums to see better. If you find you like them, then look for more original *netsuke*, those that excite the inner eye, the inner cauldron, remembering that damage and repairs have a dramatic effect on resale value, so have eagle eyes or take a magnifying glass with you!

CERAMICS

Japan's pottery history is as old as any, going back perhaps 15,000 years. These pots are not easily available as Japanese law says Neolithic items belong to the state but may be left in the custody of approved finders under certain conditions. Theoretically, you cannot buy very old pieces, but they do turn up occasionally. They may also be recent "replicas." Occasionally, one sees *haniwa* (goofy statues, often people) from ca. AD 300–400. Old *haniwa* are hard to find, though new copies abound, and this is true too of *hajiki*, a reddish earthenware for everyday and ceremonial use from the fourth century; *sueki* (Fig. 197), a gray, glass-like ware imported from Korea in the fifth century, turned on the wheel and high-fired (for centuries); and *shiki*, bisque ware bearing three-color lead glazes (*sansai*), especially in eighth-century Nara.

In contrast, fifteenth- to nineteenth-century stonewares and seventeenth- to nineteenth-century porcelains are everywhere in the West and modern pots are ubiquitous enough to be a collector's dream. So many varieties are made to such high standards at so many kilns in so many regions by so many fully and semi-professional potters today, that Japan must be the world's potting center! More potters make a living from potting in Japan than all other developed countries together (10,000–15,000 would be my estimate). The great annual exhibitions featuring carefully vetted work, and the eyes of most ceramists, suggest that the technical and artistic standards of pottery in Japan are unsurpassed.

Fig. 197

Rainbows of Shows and Skills

Artists in the West tend to be individualists, and are therefore hard to herd into large enclosures so as to provide a significant corpus of work for appraisal and judgment by keen critics and buyers. But Japan has many large exhibitions, such as the Nitten, where newcomers to the country can overview the gamut of strands and skills in Japanese pottery. Prefectures and regions also organize shows of this sort, bringing together the best-known potters of an area. Exhibitions of works by seasoned or up-and-coming potters are mounted in every season and region. In some countries, all the main shows are held in the capital or largest regional capitals. In contrast, in Japan there is a plethora of exhibitions, for example, at department stores: no matter where you live there will be interesting pottery shows to excite your interest—though the entrance fees of ¥500–1200 ($4–10) may shock.

In Japan, art is considered worth paying for, and as a result the government does little subsidizing. Outsiders find it hard to believe that art pays its way here. Galleries tend to stay in business and some artists (not only potters) even become wealthy and villages prosperous and crowded, especially during pottery fairs. Western countries should learn from Japan that there is no particular reason bankers should be rich and artists poor: success should depend on flair and hard work in any field.

It is not possible to detail here the thousands of potters working now. Instead, I mention some producing areas, giving an idea of what is made there, and a few names. A fascinating aspect of collecting, or at least learning about pottery, is that you can combine it with tourism: many kiln-rich areas are worth visiting in themselves. There is often a museum and additional general showrooms at Mashiko, Shigaraki, and Tamba-Tachikui that will prove a broader view than visiting an individual potter.

In the West, we tend to stress porcelain over stoneware or earthenware, so after explaining the difference, the reader will look at porcelain, then pottery, clearly Japanese collectors' favorite. Many are looking for personal contact with a potter at his own workshop, not a faceless porcelain factory like Noritake, however good it is.

Porcelain and Pottery Defined

True or hard-paste porcelain is made from special clay and fired at a temperature of about 2340° F (1300° C). The surface is glassy and somewhat translucent. It has a cold, hard feel to it and rings when struck. The old china made in Britain and France is called soft-paste porcelain. It has a warmer feel and is softer and lighter. It does not ring. This does not make it better or worse, just different.

Pottery in Japan is often fired to temperatures just as high as real porcelain, but is made of clays which do not ring or become transparent. Works are usually more heavily potted (the clay is less resistant to strain and knocks) and have a warmer, softer feel. These pots may be glazed (have a glassy skin) or unglazed and are termed stoneware. However, only technically minded Japanese use the word *sekki*. Most use *yakimono* as the general word for porcelain and pottery together and divide that into *jiki*, meaning "porcelain," and *tōki*, meaning "ceramics of all kinds but specially pottery."

Low-fired pottery or earthenware (*doki, tsuchimono*) is found in every land. It is light, brittle and slightly porous. The word is perfect for older pottery of Japan, such as the *haniwa* noted above, *terra cotta* or the pottery of Indonesia or Africa in general.

Fig. 198

Fig. 199

(Previous page) **Fig. 196** Imari *kraak* platter with central pomegranates, floral cartouches, ca. 1700, diam 22 in (56 cm). Author's Collection.

Fig. 197 Decorated *sueki* jar, 6th c., excavated at Nishi-Miyayama tumulus, Hyōgo Prefecture, ht 15 in (38 cm). Shoulder figurines suggest wrestling or hunting scene. Photo courtesy Kyoto National Museum.

Fig. 198 Two Imari fan-shaped plates, ca. 1880. Left: With birds, diam 9 in (23 cm). Right: With *shippō* (overlapping circles) back designs, diam 10 in (25 cm). Author's Collection.

Fig. 199 Imari porcelain four-layer *jū-bako* (food container), underglaze blue with geometric enamels and dragon on lid, ht 181/2 in (47 cm). *Tomobako* shows it was exhibited at Louisiana Purchase Exposition, 1904. Photo courtesy Flying Cranes Antiques.

Fig. 200

Fig. 201

Fig. 202

Chinese and Japanese Porcelain

China was so famous in Renaissance Europe for its beautiful ceramics that it gave its name to the ware that rich Westerners bought for their dinner services. Japan became known for porcelain in Europe from 1658 under the name Imari, the port that shipped the porcelain made at nearby but landlocked Arita.

For decades, the Dutch East India Company had danced with the Chinese traders linked to Chin-de-zhen, the center of Chinese porcelain manufacture, and ordered porcelain which they sold in Europe for high profits. When China was riven with internal dissension after the Ming Dynasty fell in 1644, supplies were cut off and the dancing stopped. Instead, the Dutch proposed to the Japanese who replaced the Chinese in the ballroom. The records of this partnership reveal that hundreds of thousands of Imari pieces were sent to Batavia (the Company's headquarters in Indonesia, now Jakarta) and Europe. This trade through Nagasaki gave great impetus to the Imari–Arita area of Kyūshū.

The Chinese perfected porcelain from the eighth to twelfth centuries. Chin-de-zhen was treasured by the emperors who gave it special orders and protection. Porcelain soon formed the bulk of China's exports to Southeast Asia. It was admired everywhere and many sought to copy it but lacked the necessary expertise and materials. Nevertheless, porcelain know-how gradually spread south to Annam and east to Korea where blue-and-white porcelain was fired in quantity during the sixteenth century.

Korean Origins of Japanese Porcelain

Toyotomi Hideyoshi officially ruled Japan from 1586 to 1598. He further unified the land after a century of civil war and infighting among the *daimyō*, and felt that one way to crown his success internally would be to conquer all or a part of Korea. His dreams ended in failure in 1598, but his generals corralled some Korean potters and drove them back to Kyūshū where they were put to work locating suitable clay. They seem to have split up and gone to different areas. The standard story says that good porcelaneous clay was found at Izumi-yama, just outside the town of Arita, in the province run by the Saga clan in west-central Kyūshū, by a Korean, Ri Sampei (Lee Sam P'yong), and porcelain was being made at Arita, probably under his guidance by 1616. However, Nagatake Takeshi (1916–87, author of *Classic Japanese Porcelain*) quotes a Nabeshima clan archive, *Arita Sarayama Daikan Nikki*, which says that Ienaga Shōemon had made porcelain at Tengudani (Arita) from 1605 and was subsequently displaced by Ri Sampei.

The Hirado clan, a little further north, also sought kaolin. In 1622, they found some and started a kiln at Mikawachi, a mere 3 miles (5 km) from Saga clan territory. Initially, there were failures and glaze materials like cobalt were a problem in the Arita area, but by the 1630s an acceptable quality was being made at several kilns. The Korean potters and others had adapted to the available materials and traditions of quite another land.

Interestingly, there were already strong traditions of stoneware in adjacent areas: Karatsu, Nakano, and Hirado were also largely started by Koreans and followed Korean patterns using coarse clay and unstable kick-wheels which resulted in irregular shapes. According to Oliver Impey, formerly of Oxford University, who has researched the early kilns, the first Imari porcelain was probably made at a kiln which also made stoneware. His book, *The Early*

Fig. 203

Fig. 204

Fig. 205

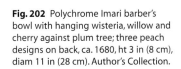

Fig. 200 Blue-and-white Imari barber's bowl with continuous flower arabesque back, ca. 1680, ht 3 in (8 cm), diam 12½ in (32 cm). Author's Collection.

Fig. 201 Polychrome Imari barber's bowl with *hanakago* (flower basket) design), bare back, 18th c., ht 3 in (8 cm), diam 10½ in (27 cm). Author's Collection.

Fig. 202 Polychrome Imari barber's bowl with hanging wisteria, willow and cherry against plum tree; three peach designs on back, ca. 1680, ht 3 in (8 cm), diam 11 in (28 cm). Author's Collection.

Fig. 203 Imari scalloped plate focusing on beribboned, collared regal cat, 19th c., width 12 in (30 cm). Photo courtesy Flying Cranes Antiques.

Fig. 204 Imari blue-and-white bowl with lid, 1860–80, ht ca. 16 in (41 cm). Private Collection.

Fig. 205 Polychrome Imari bowl with fluted rim, ca. 1950, ht 9 in (23 cm), diam 16 in (41 cm). Jay Burns Collection.

Fig. 206

Porcelain Kilns of Japan, contains a picture of a porcelain pot fused to three stoneware pots, conclusive proof that they were fired together. He believes that initially kilns kept their irons in both fires, waiting to see which product would sell best. In business terms, porcelain was an extension of their trade. This gradual changeover would explain why one cannot say which was the first porcelain kiln or who was the first porcelain potter.

Specialists call the examples of this first period and up to about 1645 Shoki-Imari, meaning "early Imari." Slightly more recent ware (up to 1700?, though some say about 1760) is Ko-Imari. This term is not precise as it literally means "old Imari."

Some less scholarly or unscrupulous dealers use this term for any "old" Imari, "old" being a question of judgment. As a personal opinion, it is unlikely that beginning collectors would want to buy Shoki-Imari. It is rather rough and ready, perhaps even coarse, and irregular in shape and color, as control of firing was still in its infancy. It is not cheap either. It is best left to specialists until you have seen a lot and are well acquainted with the subject.

A lot of the best blue-and-white Imari was made between 1650 and 1720. In a monograph sent to me analyzing the Shimada Kinji Imari Collection, Suzuta Yukio, former curator at the Kyūshū Ceramic Museum in Arita, broke the period down as follows. (There is considerable overlap and a lot of old stereotypes have to be rejected, as there is a mixture of "Old Kutani" and Kakiemon in the "Imari" fold). The first era, Jō (1650–70), had higher footrings, a thin body, deeper cobalt color, and thinner, patchy infilling (*dami*) lines, but more contrast and less refinement. The Empō or Kakiemon era (1670–90) featured refined shading and blue tones, with single large enclosed footring seals in seal script. Features of the Empō decades are white, evenly applied thin glaze. Foliate molds are common, as are brown rims, while delicate lines and "negative space with a special asymmetric placement with a special spatial tension are plentiful." The footring became vertical. Genroku era (1690–1704) Imari is less delicate, more "gorgeous" and condensed, with little negative space. Stylization is a feature. There is "gold enamel Chinese scrolling on a red ground and gold enamel on underglaze cobalt-blue. The decorative composition is segmented and filled with Chinese scrolling." After 1710, the patterns became looser and less easily defined.

Chūki Imari means "mid-period Imari"—roughly the eighteenth century, but it may cover the period 1680–1760. It has a laudatory bias, as many Japanese dealers think this is a great period, especially for blue-and-white wares made to domestic taste, as the painting is beautifully controlled, the ground clean, the shape precise, and the blue soft. Seki Kazuo, in *Seiki Imari*, suggests that the best work, perhaps including Hirado, with its precision, softness of color, and artistry has never been surpassed anywhere.

A tremendous amount of Imari porcelain left for Europe in the years 1658–1720. Later Imari lost out to lower-priced Chinese porcelain (the country had recovered stability). The European

Fig. 206 Massive Imari platter with phoenix and chrysanthemum lobes, three-colored floral designs on back and characters "Hizen Arita-Tashiro sei"—naming (Tashiro) kiln or potter is rare—ca. 1860–70, diam 22 in (56 cm). Author's Collection.

Fig. 207 Centaur plate (human face, horse body), ca. 1740, diam 10 in (25 cm). Author's Collection.

Fig. 208 *Dame au parasol* pattern plate attributed to Dutch artist Cornelius Pronk, commissioned by Dutch East India Company, ca. 1740, diam 10½ in (27 cm). Author's Collection.

Fig. 209 Imari *fūzoku* scene (showing customs): snowed-under temple with women lightening snowy boughs, rolling snowballs and readying to sweep; lots of rivers, dark trees and *fukizumi* (blowing pigment through tubes) on area round hill, decoration on back, ca. 1875, diam 18 in (46 cm). Private Collection.

Fig. 223

Fig. 224

Fig. 225

Fig. 226

Fig. 223 Imposing blue-and-white Hirado jar with *shishi* finial, body with flying cranes and sculpted dragons, 19th c., ht 15 in (38 cm). Photo courtesy Flying Cranes Antiques.

Fig. 224 Underglaze blue-and-white Hirado vase; upper body reticulated and embraced by dragons, lower part a chrysanthemum on a four-legged plinth, 19th c., ht 10 in (25 cm). Photo courtesy Flying Cranes Antiques.

Fig. 225 Rare Hirado porcelain canine family, with mother suckling, ca. 1840, ht of dog 15 1/2 in (39 cm). Photo courtesy Flying Cranes Antiques.

Fig. 226 Robust Hirado *baku* (nightmare eater); lion's body, elephant's trunk, and ox tail indicate power, 19th c., ht 8 1/2 in (22 cm). Photo courtesy Flying Cranes Antiques.

Fig. 227

Fig. 228

Kutani

This is a village on the Japan Sea coast in Fukui Prefecture in a bustling pottery area, making vividly colored ware (bright green, red, and gold are common but not blue-and-white). Plates are rarer than saké sets (often two flasks and five cups) or tea services in Western shapes. They are often marked with the easy-to-read Japanese characters "nine valleys." For over a century, Kutani has sold pretty saké sets, and collectors will find hundreds of modestly priced (from $1) items at flea markets and stores. Quite a few pieces with exotic love scenes (*shunga*) may catch your eye, or trick pieces, such as a birdsong flask which "sings" when you pour, or has a hidden tube so liquid seemingly disappears.

As explained later, Kutani was created anew so potting and painting skills were brought in; bosses vied for the best so Honda Sadakichi, Saida Isaburō, Aoya Gen'uemon, Matsuya Kikusaburō, and Kutani Shōza painted everywhere! Famous kilns are the Kasugayama, Wakasugi, Ono, Minzan, Yoshidaya, Sano, Miyamoto and Eiraku, wrote Georges Bouvier in *Daruma* 39.

The area had been famous for seventeenth-century pieces made in the unique style known as Ko-Kutani, considered to be of high artistic value. Kanazawa has a museum with many masterpieces in this style, and since most such pieces were apparently found in the Kanazawa area, it was assumed that Ko-Kutani originated there. This reputation led the Kaga clan to "restart" Kutani early in the nineteenth century. This was a difficult task as the kiln sites were unknown, apart from two old and seemingly unsuccessful kilns. What we buy today is the product of this venture (Figs. 227–231).

Fig. 227 Deep polychrome bowl with flowers and birds, painted by Takekoshi Zenbei I (1843–1907), diam 15 1/2 in (39 cm). Photo courtesy Keisei Isogaya Museum.

Fig. 228 Kutani *haisen* (saké cup rinsing bowls), c. 1890. Left: ht 7 in (18 cm). Front: Heian woman, ht 6 in (15 cm). Right: ht 6 in (15 cm). Author's Collection.

Fig. 229 Ko-Kutani style shallow porcelain bowl with magnificent bold decoration, 17–18th c., ht 2 in (5 cm), diam 13 in (33 cm). Ko-Kutani was made at Arita, Kyūshū, but long thought made near Kanazawa. Photo courtesy Kyoto National Museum.

Fig. 238   Fig. 239   Fig. 240

leaves a network of fine cracks. When designs are added, the crackling provides a built-in ground and the chance of light diffracting colors in different directions. Common are a light fawn or khaki green, often finely painted with floral and other designs.

Yabu Meizan (1853–1934) of Osaka was the most prolific manufacturer of Satsuma ware. He bought undecorated blanks from Chin Jukan of Kagoshima. He won a prize at the Kyoto Exhibition in 1885, then capitalized on international expositions to make good sales and garner enormous orders, especially from America. In the 1880s, he portrayed *rakan* (disciples of Buddha), other Buddhist themes, and Chinese children, but from the 1890s he turned to more Japanese subjects like fighting samurai or subjects copied from *ukiyo-e*. His very precise designs were made by using copper-plate designs, transferred to paper and outlined against the pottery ground.

Other famous names are Kinkōzan of Kyoto, run by Kobayashi Sohei (1867–1927), whose patterns tended to fit the shape better than Yabu Meizan's, and Takebe Shōkō, who worked with English trader T. B. Blow and Swiss collector Alfred Baur. Joe Earle mentions how the "combination of absorbing subject matter with infinitely painstaking craftsmanship exercised such a fascination among those Europeans and Americans who could afford the best work." Many other marks, like the typical "plus sign within a box" of the Shimazu family, hereditary rulers of the Kagoshima clan, can be found. As so many places made Satsuma, the painting and finish are uneven, but some Satsuma is great! Irrespective of origin, it was exported as Satsuma "Far Eastern Jewellery."

Fig. 241

Fig. 239 Globular Satsuma vase, *gosu* blue and colored enamels with panels of brocade patterns and floral motifs on pale ground of stylized waves, 19th c., ht 14 in (35 cm). Photo courtesy Flying Cranes Antiques.

Fig. 240 Satsuma vase, fan-shaped panels show ducks on lake and underwater scene on a rust red ground; shoulder bears autumn flowers and chrysanthemums; panels signed Sōzan, one marked "Kyoto, Kinkōzan zō," Meiji era, ht 8 in (20 cm). Photo courtesy Flying Cranes Antiques.

Fig. 241 Lidded Satsuma jar with detailed painting; two panels depict bow, arrow, and armor makers, adults playing *go*, and children with puppies; others bear natural subjects and Lake Biwa scenery, signed Yabu Meizan on base, Meiji era, ht 5 in (13 cm). Photo courtesy Flying Cranes Antiques.

Fig. 242

Fig. 242 *Imban* (transfer-printed plates), ca. 1880. Left: Octagonal plate with lucky gods Ebisu and Hotei, diam 12 in (30 cm). Right: Scarecrow scene, diam 6½ in (16 cm). Front: Three Shōjō atop saké vats with long ladles (*hishaku*) against a *seigaiha* ground, a design often used by the Kameyama kiln, diam 8 in (20 cm). Author's Collection.

Transfer and Stencil-Printed Porcelain

Japanese distinguish carefully between hand-painted (*tegaki*) and the less valued printed (*imbande*) porcelain (Figs. 242–245). There are several techniques. Most common are *dōban tensha* (copper-plate transfer, or decal) and *katagami imban tensha* (stencil-paper transfer print), though designs were also incised (*inkoku*). Printed china became popular in the revolutionary 1870–80s when everything was changed and people wanted novelty in every field. It had the advantage of being cheaper to make and more suited to detailed lines and therefore to depicting the new things coming in from the West, like trains and bridges and telegraph wires.

In antique stores and flea markets, it is common and inexpensive, so we use it for parties at home (very durable but heavy, though widely praised by guests, and at friends' houses in New York and Britain). I collect it and wrote the first book on it, *Igezara: Printed China*, analyzing the different forms of decoration and techniques, and showing why transfer-printing excels where detail is desirable but Japanese prefer hand-painted (as do I for fine pieces). Some pieces have transfer-printed outlines and hand-painted detail. Attractive pieces in Japan are $10–300 but often more overseas. It is undervalued and very collectible! In the long term, Bunmei Kaikaku and other exotic designs will hold/build value while standard designs may wilt.

Fig. 243

Fig. 244

Fig. 245

Fig. 243 *Igezara* (printed plates with brown pie-crust rim), late 19th c. Left: Scholar at garden gate, diam 15 in (38 cm). Front: Hawk hunting scene, diam 7 in (18 cm). Right: *Shi'itake* mushrooms, diam 81/2 in (22 cm). Author's Collection.

Fig. 244 *Imban* plates. Left: Uniformed schoolboys by waterwheel. Right: Kojima Takanori carving poem on cherry tree, roughly meaning "Heaven will not desert Your Highness; a faithful retainer will come and rescue you", ca. 1880. Author's Collection.

Fig. 245 *Imban* plates. Left: Rickshaw puller against a Mt Fuji ground with bats and plovers; *fukizumi* technique gives speckle, illegible blue mark, floral sprays on back, diam 81/2 in (22 cm).

Right: Rice bale and "Artificial Fertilizer Co." (now Tokyo Exchange quoted firm, new name), diam 8 in (20 cm). Author's Collection.

Sumidagawa

This is a colorful ware popular in the United States, made for export by the River Sumida, Tokyo, with a 1900–1920s heyday, and discontinued after the war. It is little seen in Japan, but *SUMIDA* by Herbert Karp and Gardner Pond gives a full description.

The teapots, vases, and mugs (and a million others) are often red and black, heavy, and covered with figures in relief. According to Jan-Erik Nilsson's website from Gothenburg, Sweden, "the style of applied figures on a surface with flowing glaze was invented about 1890 by the Seto potter Ryōsai I, who worked in Tokyo from about 1875 to 1900. They are often embellished with glazed plaques with handwritten signatures or general good luck symbols.... Many are probably the work of one family—Inoue Ryōsai I (1828–?), Ryōsai II (born ca. 1860) and Ryōsai III (1888–1971)." Other potters include Hara Gozan, Ishiguro Kōko, Sakurai Fuji, and Sezan. Commonly the upper half is partially flambé glazed, or glazed with two or more splashed colors that may run, creating droplets. The unglazed portion may be painted, glaze or bisque.

To give a feel for pricing, I quote a June 2003 Sotheby's London auction: "A large Sumidagawa vase, circa 1900, the turned iron-red body shaped unevenly to resemble caves and ponds on a mountain with assembled rakan, a thick black glaze covers the neck and trickles down, details in various shades of grey, green, blues and browns, signed in seal form on a white porcelain plaque Tōgyokuen Ryōsai-zō, and on a scroll held by an immortal, Sumidagawa, 47.7 cm., 18.75 in., expected price range £2,000–3,000." Smaller pieces are in the hundreds of dollars.

Mike McLeod mentions on the Net a "magnificent example by Inoue Ryōsai in the Lightner Museum in St Augustine, Fla., [which] has 354 applied monkey figures swarming over homes in a village. Another fabulous piece by Ishiguro Kōko stands 48 inches high and exhibits 500 rakan. In 1899, it won first prize in an exhibition in Tokyo, and now resides in the George Walter Vincent Smith Art Museum in Springfield, Mass." He is amazed by the detail on earlier works where eyes, lips, teeth, and even tongues are fashioned, but later just a line for the mouth.

Other names for Sumidagawa include Poo ware, Banko, and Asakusa Banko. Poo ware was made by a Shekwan potter, Poo You-she, with patterns like Sumida. The term Banko applied to Japanese export or souvenir wares. To satisfy governments, the words Nippon, Made in Japan (USA) and Foreign (UK) may be applied. A US dealer has warned me that the colors are not firm, so washing with strong detergents could strip the color.

Folkcrafts and Pottery

As a concept, folkcrafts have greater resonance than in other rich countries as industrialization started later (allowing local crafts to survive) and due to innate conservatism, the promotional movement by Yanagi Sōetsu, potters Hamada Shōji, Briton Bernard Leach, Kawaii Kanjirō and Tomimoto Kenkichi, deliberate postwar government promotion, and the custom, since 1950, of anointing experienced old craftsmen as "Living National Treasures." Yanagi's philosophy has a physical presence in the famous Mingeikan near Tokyo University, which houses his 1930s collection.

The Folkcraft Association of Japan still pushes its ideals: that craftsmen make practical items working with other artisans along traditional lines with local materials and without conscious "prettification," and sell them at low prices and unsigned.

As Brian Moeran relates in *Folk Art Potters of Japan*, this ideal is outdated. He studied Onta, a pottery village in the hills of Oita Prefecture, Kyushu, reckoned to be as near the ideal as anywhere but found it falls short. The folkcraft boom of the late 1960s and 1970s caused inequality and reduced co-operation, as city people traveled to kilns and workshops all over the countryside. On his evidence, incomes went up tenfold in Onta for many lucky craftsmen, making them solidly middle class. He found everybody knew about Yanagi (so their work could not be unconscious) and saw that his ideals were impractical as uniform goods did not sell but new ones did. Why make uniform goods when locals, wholesalers, city folk, and the craftsmen themselves all favor different pots?

Folkcrafts have been made in every land and some, like Moroccan leather, Toledo steel or damascene, are internationally famous, but other factors explain its resonance here. As Moeran says, the ideals are close to those of traditional rural society. Just as William Morris's yearning to go back to old hand-worked traditions in his British movement came some 100 years after the Industrial Revolution, so Yanagi harked after the old rural life that was crumbling around him, inspired by Leach's comments on Morris.

The clan system of Japan hurt the individual but built local strengths. Fiefs had some economic independence and vied to sell to others and keep secret their own successful goods. For example, once you were employed at the Nabeshima kiln (see page 125), you had to stay forever while would-be apprentices from outside were turned away in case they were really industrial spies (often true, as with the spread of Imari skills to Seto and Tohoku). Indigo (*ai*) was the local product of Tokushima, Shikoku; the clan made the production process a secret to uphold an exclusive aura and so the indigo price when trading with other fiefdoms. Even now, the Ishikawa Prefectural Museum refuses to accept that "old Kutani" was made in Kyushu, so that it can proclaim the uniqueness of its "Old Kutani" collection (anyway the pots are fabulous and worth traveling thousands of miles to see, so it is easy to see why the pots which were mainly found in the area acquired the aura of myth).

The poor transport system into the twentieth century (Hida Takayama was only linked by rail to the outside world in the 1930s) also kept alive the tradition of local crafts longer than in many advanced countries. This was bolstered by the old Japanese urge to tag each area as being "famous" for a certain good or scene, as in *ukiyo-e* print sets. Then, travel books gave the special textiles or dolls of towns along the Tōkaidō Highway (Osaka–Edo). The buying of special local food or crafts when traveling is still very strong. When teachers from my university proctor entrance exams in faraway places, they bring back the local cookies or cakes for other teachers.

Lively stories reflect this tradition. Some men may tell their wives about a forthcoming business trip, spend a night with a lady friend, and next day buy for their wife an *omiyage* (souvenir) of the region they pretended to visit at the concourse of Osaka Station (where every prefecture has a store selling its traditional crafts or foods) to "prove" they made the business trip.

The Craft Business

Folkcrafts (like dolls and woodcrafts) appear in other chapters but the theory and practices of pottery given here apply there too.

The Prefectural Craftgoods Association of Japan has a large hall in Aoyama, Tokyo, where the crafts of each region are displayed and craftsmen can sometimes be seen at work and admired; regions still

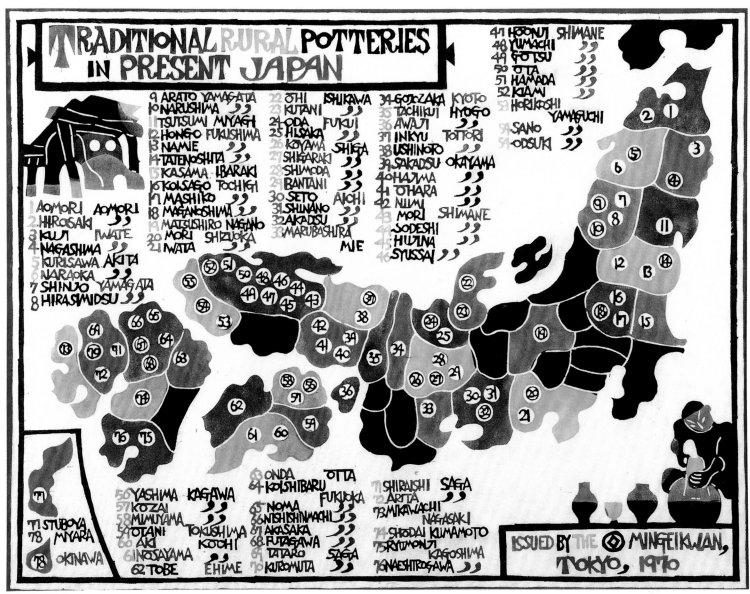

Fig. 246

uphold their distinctive flavor, for prestige and economic reasons.

The internet page of the Folkcraft Association of Japan lists 191 local crafts under the categories of weaving, dyeing, ceramics, lacquer, wood, bamboo, metal, paper, writing materials, Buddhist altars, and miscellaneous. This last includes Ise stencils, Izumo stone lanterns, Marugame fans, Kōshū deerskin and crystal carving, Banshū fish flies and abacuses, and dolls from Hakata, Edo, Kyoto, Miyagi, and Suruga—a veritable rainbow.

Japanese Crafts: A Complete Guide to Today's Traditional Handmade Objects edited by Diane Durston, has beautiful photos of 91 fine traditional crafts and a welter of additional information. It mentions the various techniques but avoids saying directly that they are folkcraft, as the items she has selected are refined; they are the BMWs, not the Chevvies of this world. In her introduction, she says that in the 1990s the Japan Craft Forum identified 1,060 "distinctive crafts" made by over 240,000 craftspeople, of which 184 have been granted official government recognition.

Collecting Folkcraft

As can be seen above, local crafts have an importance far outweighing that in other advanced countries—which makes tourism all the more enjoyable. However, if collecting crafts means spend-

ing a lot of money, collectors should be on guard. There is a great vested interest in maintaining the system, but it is hard to decide whether the "crafts" have not become industries underpinning tourism and local economies,

When buying cheap things while traveling, this does not matter, but before deciding to collect things which cost real money, collectors should ask themselves whether they are buying something made by an individual craftsman with his/her own idiosyncrasies and skills, or a mass-produced industrial product that might have little resale value. On the contrary putting together a collection, for example of dolls or saké flasks from each place you visit, can provide a lot of satisfaction, while keeping old memories alive.

Given the number and variety of items mentioned already, it would be silly to put forward certain items as being particularly

Fig. 246 Mingeikan map of traditional potteries in Japan, Tokyo, 1970. Tsuda Yoshio Collection.

Fig. 247

Fig. 248

Fig. 249

collectable, but I shall add that the materials you like (I love woods with strong grains, while my wife prefers paper and textiles) will probably influence what you collect. If you get the chance to visit a hall exhibiting all kinds of things, take the plunge and look around. If you buy nothing, at the least you will have received a general education and you just might find some aspect that fascinates you! Whatever happens, you get an insight into the pride and workmanship of the Japanese artisan. For them, money matters less than using and passing on skills handed down from the past, and always aiming at perfection—though making a living matters too, of course.

If forced to define where collecting is feasible, I would stutter and say that creativity within a tradition, expensive materials that have been carefully chosen, and proof of authorship are factors that matter, like clear tactile qualities, durability, and possible utility. Having shot off that bolt, collecting attractive or interesting things is the endearing habit of every magpie and squirrel, so why not you? Find out if you are a kleptomane by looking. Pottery might be your thing!

Pottery Areas: The Six Ancient Kilns

Pottery (*tōki*) is made everywhere in Japan, so let us start with the Six Ancient Kilns (see pottery map Fig. 246) which had started in the Middle Ages and survived the centuries: Bizen, Tamba, Shigaraki, Seto, Echizen, and Tokoname. Two dozen others made pots but gained less fame, so do not count historically.

Bizen

Bizen ware (Figs. 247, 248) has been made at Imbe Village, Okayama Prefecture, for 800 years and may be the most distinct and conservative. After a 200-year slump, it was revived by Kaneshige Tōyō in the 1930s. It uses clay from below rice fields, and largely avoids glazes. It looks old-fashioned or heavy when you first meet it, but grows on you with time. The colors are restrained (browns and reds are common) and the bottom surface is somewhat gritty due to inclusions (fine when placed on tatami mats but hard on polished furniture with no mats). Bizen sometimes uses straw (*hidasuki*) or leaves to apply marks to a pot's surface during firing and leave a permanent imprint, which can be beautiful. Bizen ware is fired for 10–14 days, using large quantities of pinewood, which explains why a saké thimble often costs $50. Some 350 potters are said to be active and the town is prosperous. Kakurezaki Ryūichi (1950–) is some people's favorite, while critic Robert Yellin believes Harada Shūroku (Fig. 249), Mori Tōgaku, and Abe Anjin make the most exciting pots, while upholding Momoyama traditions. Other notables are Fujiwara Yū, Fujiwara Kei, and Yamamoto Tōshū.

Tamba

Tamba ware (Fig. 254) comes from Tachikui in the hills behind Kobe. Prominent designs include a vertical prawn (which is strange as Tachikui is located inland!), farming vats and, more recently, saké jars with dripped writing on them advertising a store or brewery. Tamba's location made it hard to ship finished pots to coastal markets. Most potters in the village are surnamed Ichino or Shimizu, so go by their first names.

There is a museum in the nearby castle town of Sasayama and a collection of materials in the village of Tachikui (Figs. 250–254), which give a good historical overview. As in Bizen, Tamba potters did not use glaze but used the natural ash glaze from the pine logs burnt in the kiln. The effect of this "glaze" cannot be planned exactly, so luck is needed to make things turn out well. Unexpected, admired results of firing are called *yōhen*.

The names Bizen and Tamba reflect the province where they are located. Both areas found favor with those who founded the Tea cult and admired the pots' simplicity and quiet unpretentiousness. Orders from Kyoto helped build up the kilns in the late sixteenth century. Both passed through bad times when industrialization threatened them, but flourish, thanks largely to the Mingei Movement that valued nameless potters over those with famous seals.

Fig. 250

Fig. 251

Fig, 247 Bizen flask for medical saké (sweet, with herbs), ca. 1850, ht 7 in (18 cm). Author's Collection.

Fig. 248 Bizen storage jar, Muromachi era, ca. 1480. Photo courtesy Montgomery Collection.

Fig. 249 Bizen stoneware. Middle: Rectangular plate with frame, length 12 in (30 cm), width 7 1/2 in (19 cm). Left, on tray: saké server, ht 5 in (13 cm). Back: Vase by Kimura Koraku-en, ht 9 in (23 cm). Back right: Spouted serving bowl, diam 5 in (13 cm). Right: Two unglazed saké cups by Yoshimoto

Tadashi; saké cup with white inside (Tamba) by Ikuta Tazutaka (1927–82), Tsuda Yoshio Collection; pale saké cup with typical *hidasuki* red and brown flame pattern by Kyoko, daughter of Yamamoto Tōshū at Bishū kiln ca. 1975. Front: Three-footed, two-leaf cake dish by Harada Shūroku, ca. 1980, length 9 in (23 cm). Author's Collection.

Fig. 250 Large green Tamba plate by Ichino Satoru, ca. 1978, diam 18 1/2 in (47 cm). Author's Collection.

Fig. 251 Tamba stoneware large, deep plate by Shibata Masa'aki (1950–), unsigned, diam 15 in (38 cm). Tsuda Yoshio Collection.

Fig. 252

Fig. 253

Fig. 254

Shigaraki

This is an area south of Lake Biwa and east of Kyoto. From the late twelfth century, it made high-fired pots with some "hot spots" receiving a natural ash glaze. It features distinctive clay with glassy beads of quartz and feldspar embedded in it. The area runs a regular international pottery festival, turns out huge amounts of utilitarian and garden pieces like planters, and is known for its *tanuki.*

The real animal is a badger or raccoon dog associated with good luck and money. The statues come in all sizes, from doll to mammoth, and are bisexual with breasts and prominent gonads. A large wallet and saké flask complete the *tanuki*'s kit. Many years ago two young male students gave my wife a *tanuki* when she told them about our engagement. It still stands at our front door though it needs a nose job after falling in the Kobe earthquake. Perhaps it saved the house and family.

Seto

Seto (Fig. 257) is a general name for the area north of Nagoya. The word *setomono,* literally "thing from Seto," means china, as this area has made much of the country's tableware for centuries. To emphasize that Seto is the heartland of Japanese pottery, the term *Kuniyaki* ("national ware" is sometimes applied to its output.

The biggest medieval base was probably around Mt Sanage, turning out glazed blackish-brown and yellowish-green vases and ordinary crockery. Later kilns were known for coarse, yellow, horse-eye plates (*Ki-Seto*) (Fig. 256). The area is closely associated with the tea ceremony as many tea masters patronized it or came from there. Plentiful china clays are found in Seto and its surrounding districts, like Mino. The area now houses major firms making items such as basins and toilets, still using clay as the basic material.

Fig. 252 Contemporary stoneware by Shimizu Toshihiko. Left: Large *katakuchi* (spouted bowl), ht 4 in (10 cm), diam 10 1/2 in (27 cm). Right: *Mentori* (faceted) vase, height 6 in (15 cm). Front: Serving dish, unsigned. Tsuda Yoshio Collection.

Fig. 253 Tamba stoneware by Ikuta Kazutaka. Left: Fluted vase, ht 6 in (15 cm). Back: Globular vase, ht 6 in (15 cm). Right: Bowl with fluted sloping sides, diam 9 in (23 cm). Front: bowl with fluted straight sides, diam 10 in (25 cm), all 1970s, unsigned. Tsuda Yoshio Collection.

Fig. 254 Tamba jar, natural ash glaze, late 15th c., ht 17 1/2 in (44 cm). Pleasant shape from coiling, then compacting. Photo courtesy Kyoto National Museum.

Fig. 255

Fig. 256

Tokoname and Echizen

Tokoname (Fig. 258) and Echizen are no longer so active. The first is east and south of Nagoya on the Chita Peninsula and the latter at Oda-chō and Miyazaki, Fukui Prefecture. Their wares were mainly workmanlike and practical, heavy and sturdy.

Kumano Kuroemon of Echizen is popular among friends, as he tries to go beyond the boundary by firing at 1500–1700° C (2700–3000° F), creating many martyrs and an occasional hero!

Other Old Pottery Areas

Karatsu

A port near Imari and north of Arita, Karatsu had many Korean potters; Handōgame is reckoned to have been the first kiln in the mid-sixteenth century. A century later, probably some 100 kilns were making rough-hewn stoneware pots with simple underglaze floral or reed patterns, often with iron oxide painting. Karatsu varieties include *e-Garatsu* (pellucid glaze over metal glaze pictures); *madara* (speckled with blue straw-ash glaze spots); *Chōsen* (Korean style with straw ash glaze); *oku-Kōrai* (simple unprettied ware); *ki*, *ao*, and *kuro-Karatsu* (yellow, green, and black ware respectively); and *hori* or carved Karatsu. Plain Karatsu is *muji-Karatsu*.

In 1976, Nakazato Tarōemon XII (1895–1985), whose family dates from the early days, was made a Living National Treasure to recognize his reinvigoration of the ancient tradition, now carried on by his eldest son. The autumn 2002 exhibition at the Nezu Institute of Arts, Tokyo, opened people's eyes to the ancient but non-stereotypical wares, featuring much greater size, colorfulness, and the pine motif. It is particularly loved by Tea people. *Karatsumono* means china in western Japan (*setomono* in the east).

Fig. 257

Fig. 255 Seto stoneware by Mizuno Hanjirō XIII of Hongyō Gama, Seto, 1970–90. Back left: Plate, diam 8 in (20 cm). Back middle: Single flower vase, ht 9½ in (24 cm). Back right: Plate, diam 14 in (35 cm). Front left: Plate, diam 10½ in (27 cm). Front right: Bowl, ht 3 in (8 cm), diam 8 in (20 cm). Tsuda Yoshio Collection.

Fig. 256 Seto horse-eye stoneware shallow bowls, unsigned. Right: Early 20th c., diam 14 in (35 cm). Left: Late 19th c., diam 10½ in (27 cm). Tsuda Yoshio Collection.

Fig. 257 Pitcher in "Meiping" shape, Seto ware, natural ash glaze, 13–14th c., ht 7½ in (19 cm), diam 6 in (15 cm). Nice lines and glaze suggest dead leaves. Photo courtesy Kyoto National Museum.

Fig. 258

Agano

Pots from Agano date from the early seventeenth century, when the Kokura (northern Kyūshū) clan leader, Hosokawa Tadaoki, a Tea fan with many admirers, asked a Korean potter to come and built him a *noborigama* or climbing kiln in Agano. Kobori Enshū (a *daimyō* Tea master) liked many Agano bowls and other tea ceremony items. Pottery critic Robert Yellin likes its coloring, surfaces, luster, lightness, firing changes, and the way the glazes run.

Takatori

Near Fukuoka, Takatori was founded by Korean potters in 1601 and lasted 250 years, thanks in part to Kuroda *daimyō* support. It was influenced by Karatsu and at first tended to produce thickly potted everyday wares and a few tea wares. After getting orders from Kobori Enshū, the potters made slim-walled, subtler bowls with a toffee-colored glaze.

Onta

Onta is a small Kyūshū village with many admirers. In Oita Prefecture's hills (west of Beppu Spa), it keeps to the old ways of firing with wood and is marked by the style you see in Fig. 259. Observers like Moeran see it as the last bastion of folkcraft in Japan, but even he admits it is infiltrated by commercial considerations. It still usually sticks to non-signing but is self-conscious with so much to read and knows some pots sell and others do not.

Fig. 259

Hagi

This is a western Honshū castle town famous for warrior politicians in the mid- and late nineteenth century and the potters it has boasted since the Korean brothers Ri Shakkō and Ri Kei first fired Hagi around 1604 in Matsumoto-Nakanokura. The Saka and Miwa families have dominated Hagi since shortly after its founding, Miwa Kyūsetsu XI being particularly famous. The clay is generally light in color and weight, and white glazes are common. After many years of holding hot water, the surface develops a crackling which is loved especially by Tea people. Another typical trait is the "broken" base deriving from Korea. Perhaps to prevent heat deformation, potters made a triangular cut in the base that is now almost a trademark. *Ido-jawan* came from fifteenth-century Korea where they were rice bowls but Tea masters liked their quiet beauty.

Akahada

This town is associated with Nara and Yamato-Kōriyama Castle whose owner in the eighteenth century, Yanagisawa Gyōzan, invited Kyoto artists to pot in his fief and protected their market. It is delicately potted, so brittle, and often white with a pink tinge.

Iga Ueno

This was a rather rough looking, mainly domestically used form of pottery in the late sixteenth century, till tea masters Furuta Oribe and Kobori Enshū took an interest in its characteristic splits and cracks, turning it more to tea wares. Iga output slowed toward 1700 and petered out later, though output has been restarted (Fig. 260).

Mino Ceramics

Mino ceramics are stonewares from the Seto and Mino areas of Gifu Prefecture, north of Nagoya, dating from the late sixteenth century. They are tea ceremony allies. Mino-born Furuta Oribe (1544–1615) was a *daimyō* under Oda Nobunaga, Toyotomi Hideyoshi, and Tokugawa Ieyasu (who later ordered his *seppuku* for political meddling). After studying with Sen Rikyū, Oribe started his own less restrained way, teaching it to Ieyasu's son, and had tea wares made with green copper glaze, white slip, deformed shapes, and impromptu underglaze designs. Orders to seven kilns have linked them to him ever since, including some in Kyūshū. His most famous disciples are Kobori Enshū and artist Hon'ami Kōetsu. While traditional Oribe is green (Fig. 262), black also exists.

Shino

Dating from the sixteenth century, Shino tends to be white-glazed stoneware with iron oxide brush markings. It may have small pinholes in the surface, which tea masters favor as *yuzuhada* (citron skin). While valid, I see icing over gingerbread. Shino often uses milky-white ash/feldspar glaze. Varieties include *nezumi* (mouse), plain, red, pink, and pictorial Shino (*muji*, *aka*, *beni*, and *e*).

Fig. 260

Fig. 258 Tokoname figure, ca. 1800. Photo courtesy Montgomery Collection.

Fig. 259 Back: Onta (also Onda) seed storage jar, unsigned, ca. 1978, ht 14 in (35 cm). Left: Serving dish, diam 10 1/2 in (27 cm). Front: *Soba* bowl, diam 8 in (20 cm). Right: Recent saké flask, marked Onta, ht 11 in (28 cm). Typical *tobi-kan'-na* chattering on all. Tsuda Yoshio Collection. Onta saké flask Author's Collection.

Fig. 260 Iga Ueno stoneware by Tanimoto Mitsuo, with typical ash glaze, 1980s. Above: Dish, diam 8 1/2 in (22 cm). Below: Dish, diam 11 in (28 cm). Tsuda Yoshio Collection.

Fig. 261

Fig. 262

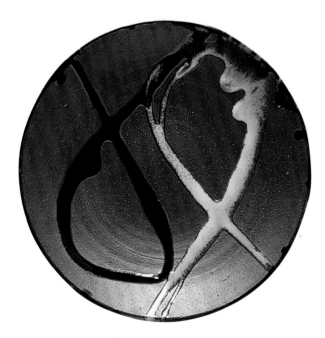

Fig. 263

Kuro-Seto

This comes from pulling pots from the kiln when still untouchably hot so that they interact with the air and turn black. Most other Seto is *ki-Seto*—yellowish to green.

Mashiko

This is located in Tochigi, northeast of Tokyo. It is home now to 300–400 mostly folkcraft-style potters and is the ceramic town closest to the capital, so thronged with tourists, kilns, and would-be potters. Ōtsuka Keizaburō probably started Mashiko in 1853. The award-winning German ceramist Gerd Knaepper started there and lives nearby. The local clay is not ideal for potting and it is really only Hamada Shōji (1894–1978) (Fig. 263) and his pupil Shimaoka Tatsuzō (Fig. 261) that made Mashiko known.

Mashiko pottery exemplified the simple, rustic charm of *mingei*, or folk art, in which craftsmen work without artistic aim or pretence to create functional objects of beauty. Utilizing nearby mountain clay and firing red pine wood, Mashiko potters speak to both the spiritual and practical sides of life with such everyday items as plates, bowls, and tea cups. Hamada was designated a Living National Treasure by the Japanese government in 1955 and Shimaoka Tatsuzō, Hamada's apprentice for three years, received the same honor in 1996.

Miyajima, who apprenticed with Shimaoka for five years, continues the *mingei* tradition. Veri, a native of Ohio, moved to Mashiko in 1982 to pursue her interest in Hamada's pottery, and she and Miyajima later established their own kiln in the area. The two artists continue to work closely together while maintaining their own styles, blending modern and traditional pottery.

Star Potters of the Twentieth Century

To choose some recent generation potters out of the thousands possible, I am going to save myself apoplexy and rely on Yono Fuyuhiko, who in a series lasting several years in *Daruma* magazine, gave his choice of Japan's best potters; many were made living national treasures (LNT), like Tamura Kōichi (1918-87) who made a name for himself with Rimpa-style designs but later added "iron painting, copper-red coating and gosu to celadon" and "devitrified white glazed or unglazed earthenware."

An *enfant terrible* is Katō Tōkurō (1897–1985), a technical genius born to a Seto potter. In a 1933 book, *Yellow Seto*, he doubted its Seto origin, posited a Mino origin, and "criticized the unfounded worship of tradition." In pre-war Japan, the idea of an unbroken line of emperors was strong: this book was seen as insulting "the ceramic ancestors", leading to some book-burning.

He got into hot water again in 1960. A saké bottle from an old Seto site was said to date from around 1300, was made "an important cultural property," but it proved later to be Tōkurō's work. This forgery scandal caused a public problem and made the experts

Fig. 261 Mashiko stoneware. Back middle: Soy sauce pitcher by Shimaoka Tatsuzō (LNT), ca. 1970, ht 4 in (10 cm). Back right: Triangular vase by Shimaoka Tatsuzō, ht 7 1/2 in (19 cm). Front right: Square plate by Shimaoka Tatsuzō, diam 7 1/2 in (19 cm). Back left: Small black plate by Hamada Shōji's pupil(s)?, 1970s, diam 5 in (13 cm). Front left: Large black plate by Hamada Shōji's pupil(s)?, 1970s, diam 10 in (25 cm). Tsuda Yoshio Collection.

mad, but it also showed his virtuoso technical proficiency. His art name, Ichimusai, implied we all start from scratch in each generation, as he believed in "*ichidai kagiri*, only one generation, so hereditary tradition is invalid." After being famous in youth for his Shino *Tsurara* (Icicle) and Oribe works, he later delivered a well-received ceramic wall to China. In his last decade, he focused on perfecting a *murasaki* (purple) Shino.

The reputation of Fujimoto Yoshimichi (1919–92, LNT) rests on his polychrome porcelain which used original methods, like mixing pigments (for a wide color range) that all melted at the same heat. Instead of outlining colors and filling them in, pigments themselves formed colors' light and shade, allowing greater realism and painterliness. He achieved great success: he was first President of the Tokyo National University of Fine Arts and Music.

Opinions about Kitaōji Rosanjin (1883–1959) are as the ocean. From an adopted but priestly Kyoto background, he grew up independent enough to study Japanese painting, calligraphy, antiques, ceramics, lacquer, and cooking on his own, then opened swish restaurants that attracted the rich. He had a knack for making food look good and asked Kita Kamakura potters to make dishes which he decorated with literary (for example, haiku) allusions. Thus he was not a potter in the narrow sense (so fakes abound) but his name is magic in Japan! (The land's two greatest gods are Convenience and Epicureanism.)

Katō Hajime (1900–68) was a Seto potter and great technician who spent years researching the clay base (*soji*) of pots and their glazes and was awarded the Grand Prize at the Paris International Exposition in 1937. He developed new overglazing techniques. He died trying to finish a large ceremonial jar for the emperor.

In a way, Arakawa Toyozō (1894–1985), LNT, rediscovered Shino when in 1930 he chanced upon old kilns in the Mino hills. He worked hard to recreate the old Shino glazes, softening them and sometimes combining them with Karatsu style iron patterns.

After a promising start and prizes with the traditionalist Japan Ceramic Association 1966–8 and an assured future, Kamoda Shōji (1933–83) (Fig. 264) suddenly moved to Tōno in northern Japan and changed to simple ash-glazed pottery with incised patterns, color inlays, straw-rope patterns, and primary colors.

It is clear that Hamada Shōji (1894–1978, LNT, see Fig. 263) will be a big name for centuries. He helped Bernard Leach set up a kiln in Cornwall, UK, and spent three years there opening his eyes to other old traditions—slipware and pitchers—that also spurred his activity in the Mingei Movement (later he headed the Mingeikan). He single-handedly made Mashiko a potting center, gave it study resources, and taught Shimaoka Tatsuzō, his artistic son. Yono says: "Earlier he liked rich, chocolate colours with contrasting light slip decoration, applied like a master, though he also did darker slip on creamy browns. In mid-life he turned more to greys and green glazes. Later there was more variety and the use of characters. His trade mark colour was persimmon."

Fig. 264

Fig. 262 Fan-shaped lidded green Oribe box with three legs and handle, Mino (Oribe); spatula applied fan decoration and rustic *sabi-e* painting, 16th c., ht 4½ in (11 cm), length 12 in (30 cm), width 10 in (25 cm). Photo courtesy Kyoto National Museum.

Fig. 263 Stoneware plate by Hamada Shōji (1894–1978), ca. 1970. Photo courtesy Montgomery Collection.

Fig. 264 Contemporary stoneware by Hamada Shōji's pupils. Top: Pouring flask by Kamoda Shōji, ht 7 in (18 cm). Center: Two-eared vase by Fuji'i Sachiko, ht 8 in (20 cm). Below: Vase by Fuji'i Sachiko, ht 7 in (18 cm). Tsuda Yoshio Collection.

Fig. 266

Fig. 265

Fig. 267

Studio Potters

The term "studio potter" is relatively new and evokes various reactions. Defining it is easiest by opposites: a traditional Djerba (Tunisia) potter making the wares handed down on the island for centuries, and the ordinary folkcraft potter of Japan, are the exact opposite of studio potters; both traditional artists make things in the old shapes for use on the table and are not concerned with developing new items or making ornaments.

Studio potters, on the other hand, try to use all the resources of knowledge, their own imagination, and other cultures' traditions to make new things that may be useful but are also akin to sculpture in some way. They are an expression of his/her desire to express and create anew—like Basil Cardew, Bernard Leach, Lucie Rie, and Hans Coper in Britain, and Peter Voulkos and Robert Turner in the US: they do not fit Biblical definitions of potters, yet have added immeasurably to mankind's achievements.

Various traditional forms of ceramics in Japan have been outlined above, but the whole current of the times is towards originality and self-expression, so that the generalizations apply to the past, but who can foretell the future? In any case, the "traditional Mashiko style" of Hamada and Shimaoka, to take an extreme example, may have been lost in the feverish experimentation that busies the kilns there now that "let 1000 flowers bloom."

The Mingei Kyōkai tries hard to keep alive potting within a certain tradition, playing down personal creativity and selfishness, and upholding the tradition of anonymity, as does their local representative in Hyogo Prefecture, Shimizu Toshihiko (see Fig. 252); but the same artist holds individual exhibitions at famous department stores and is happy to sell there at prices that reflect the public's evaluation of his ability. In a sense, folkcraft and an advanced economy with plentiful information cannot co-exist.

Fig. 265 Vase with design of irises by Makuzu Kōzan, early 20th c., ht 4 1/2 in (11 cm). Photo courtesy Oriental Treasure Box.

Fig. 266 Curling lipped stoneware vessel with brilliant poppies by Makuzu Kōzan; *tomobako*, Meiji era, ht 12 in (30 cm). Photo courtesy Flying Cranes Antiques.

Fig. 267 High-shouldered, waisted porcelain vase enameled in yellow, incised with butterflies on leaves, signed Seifū Yohei III on base, *tomobako*, Meiji era, ht 12 1/2 in (32 cm). Photo courtesy Flying Cranes Antiques.

suke, his son, and concentrated on studying Chinese, Korean, and modern European ceramics. The fruits of this are seen in Song Dynasty (960–1279) style celadon and other works, duly noted on the base or accompanying box (*tomobako*). Remember that such statements mean "inspired by" or "in the style of"—they were not copies! *Makuzu Kōzan sei* is the commonest base mark. Makuzu II suggests a twentieth-century date. Called Miyagawa Kōzan in Japan, Makuzu Kōzan's studio had a very large production, is extremely collectible and pricey at auction (see Figs. 265, 266, 270, 271)!

Another popular studio potter is third-generation Kyoto ceramist Seifū Yohei III (1851–1914) (Figs. 267, 268). Because he mainly served the Japanese market, many of the pieces sold there are 6 inches (15 cm) or less in height though pieces in foreign hands are commonly a foot or more (exceptional is the 18 inch (45 cm) white vase shown by Spink in 1990) but he was also well known abroad through expositions. In addition to the interest in Chinese styles imbibed "intravenously" by Kyoto potters, he achieved monochromes unseen anywhere. Deeply respected in Japan, he was the first potter appointed to the Imperial Arts Commission (1893). He used a short mark reading *Seifū* ("pure wind"). Perhaps one might say his pots were more restrained and self-effacing than the rather in-your-face Makuzu Kōzan, but both had ceramic and painterly skills of the highest order.

Close to the market (mostly peopled by "Victorians"), Makuzu also made fussy pots around 1881 with incrusted designs that personally I regret, such as doves and cherries in high relief on vases (see Figs. 13–22 in *Miyagawa Kōzan*). Other known studio potter names include Inoue Ryōsai, Fukugawa Eizaimon, Katō Tomotarō, Suwa Sosan II (famous for celadon and asked by Korea for guidance in reviving this old Korean staple), and Itō Tōzan.

Foreign Potters in Japan

Bernard Leach has been revered within Japan since the 1920s (and recently in the UK!) as a seminal artist and potter on a par with the other greats of the Mingei Movement. Readers are referred to the great Exhibition catalogue of the British Museum (1980).

Daruma has covered the work of three non-Japanese potters, including Richard Milgrim (1955–), who mainly makes tea wares in Shino, Karatsu, Oribe, Seto, and Hagi styles. He has one foot now in the Kyoto countryside and another in the US.

Gerd Knaepper is German but has spent thirty years in and around Mashiko. He is famous for winning the Grand Prize of the Education and Culture Minister for traditional Japanese Ceramics (the first vetted anonymously and so without bias) in 1971 (his second year as a potter), rebuilding Tarōsaka Manor at Daigo with ox-eye dormer windows so hauntingly it has graced *Architectural Digest*, and for winning public commissions to sculpt works in clay and metal to adorn bridges, tunnels, and open spaces—as well as Botticelli Venus-type shell figures and torsos (see *Daruma* 30).

Edward Hughes went to art schools in England, then spent similarly seminal time in Kyoto before setting up a kiln on the shores of Lake Biwa and building a reputation for combining some of the great traditions of England, like slipware patterns, with the professional standards of Japan. From his current English Lake District home, he visits Japan regularly with his wife Shizuko for sales at department stores, so keeps a foot in both camps and his old customers happy. He uses Shigaraki-like clay with admixtures and has many admirers.

Advice to Collectors

Japanese consider dining important; it should take place in appropriate surroundings with attractive receptacles. Lacquerware was important (see Lacquerware) but not silver. Porcelain was vital for the rich and gradually expanded its market among the middle classes. Some porcelain critics say poorer painting started ca. 1760 as demand rose and standards slipped. Porcelain only reached the poorer classes in the Meiji era. Tea people and the more intellectual folk valued all kinds of stoneware, such as Bizen and Shigaraki, but the main thrust of polite society was lacquer and porcelain.

Westerners like same-pattern dinner sets, but the Japanese prefer many different shapes and patterns. At a *kaiseki* meal (formal and traditional in high-class restaurants), some 30 dishes will be placed before the guests—all differing in style and shape. People love the heavenly variety of colors, shapes, and motifs to complement the tastes dreamed up for the seasonal materials. You may want to follow this penchant and buy "non-sets."

If the porcelain you buy is dirty or stained, the first step is to wash it with ordinary detergent and a brush. If this is insufficient, use a powder scouring agent as it is more abrasive. Really stubborn stains may be taken out with bleach, but be careful to apply it only to the area in question. If you leave a dish for days in bleach, overglaze colors may go or cracks could grow into chasms. Sometimes tissue soaked in bleach and left directly only over a stain works well.

Normally, the Japanese like to repair with visible gold and silver whereas the British prefer invisible mending. For Japanese, gold mends suggest an owner cared enough to spend money, but you may prefer not to see the repair. Price and quality vary widely, so ask around and get a firm quote beforehand. On a dish bought for ¥10,000 ($85), a restorer asked ¥30,000 for a repair I did not like!

It is acceptable to ask the dealer if a piece has any cracks or mends. If reputable, (s)he will answer honestly and write the opinion as well. If you spend quite a lot on a piece or a set (five or ten in Japan), my advice is to get the dealer to record its condition, period, and area of production, with a view to holding him responsible if it is false. Of course if he writes in Japanese and you cannot read it, he may still fool you. An experienced dealer colleague bought a large bowl deep in the countryside, thinking that the chit written by the dealer said "Made in the Meiji era." It did not. It said "It is marked as being made in the Meiji era"—not the same thing at all! It had been made recently and given a Meiji mark.

Another note about marks: old porcelain often has "fake" reign marks like *Dai Ming Seika Nensei*. This literally means "made in China during the Seika reign of the Great Ming Dynasty." However, this should not be taken seriously. A better conclusion is the Japanese kiln wanted the onlooker to compare it with such famous porcelain. In this sense, marks on the base are meaningless. Other common ones are *fuku* and *kotobuki*, both wishing good fortune.

To assist with dating, it may be helpful to know that the term Dai Nippon Teikoku (Empire of Greater Japan) was made the official name of the country in 1889 and rejected after World War II for its militaristic overtones. The term *Dai Nihon/Nippon* was used since olden times to refer to important aspects of the country's history, so it is not as accurate a marker: *Teikoku* is defining.

"Made in Occupied Japan" (often poorly printed), sometimes seen on the bottom of, for example, plates indicates a date between 1945 and April 1952, when the US Occupation ended. Americans collect work with this mark, as seen in *Schiffer's Book for Collectors*.

FURNITURE

Traditional Japanese furniture is a new world: novel shapes, patterns, grains, and metalwork make this field very special. The aesthetic is somewhat severe (workmanlike might be a better term) and much less "pretty" than, for example, lacquerware, but as you will see, the solidity of the wooden panels (not veneer) and the extensive corner ironwork mark furniture out as a field that will run—for generations.

Several distinguishing marks come to mind. The objectives and so the shapes of traditional Japanese furniture are miles away from London or New York. While gun cupboards certainly exist in the West, they are not something we would drool over as beautifully made (the Purdy or Winchester in it is a different story) nor write our names all over them, unlike the sword chest which was often lovingly and proudly inscribed. The ship's and wheeled chests are other examples where the Japanese championed impregnable but portable strength for marine purposes or maneuverability (mainly to escape fire)—situations unlikely to face middle- or upper-class Westerners—nor indeed do we use furniture to go upstairs.

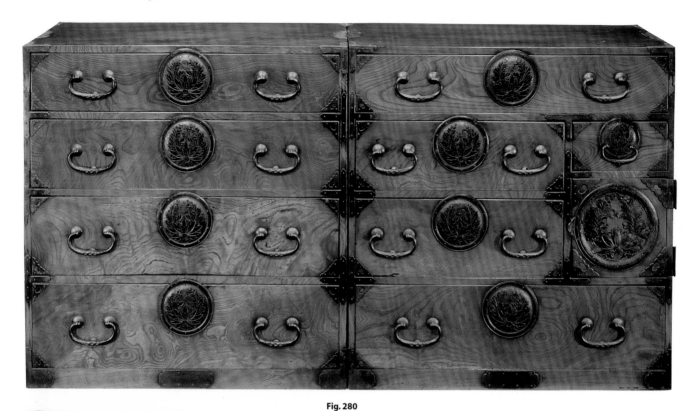

Fig. 280

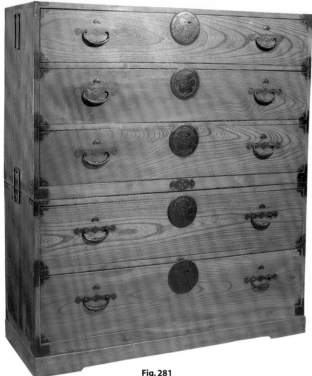

Fig. 281

Fig. 282

Early History of Furniture

Before 1600, only prominent people in Japan owned furniture, usually a few *hitsu* or wooden containers and *nagamochi* (lidded trunks). Others had closets for extra bedding and their few clothes. Peace, however, brought prosperity and from the late seventeenth century richer merchants owned a few chests. During the eighteenth century, ownership became more general, as we can see from woodblock prints. But there were innumerable fires and most furniture you see for sale today was made after 1850.

The Meiji era (1868–1912) was a great watershed. Before this time, Japan was a feudal country scarcely linked to the outside world. Later, it became the leading power in the East, having defeated China and Russia in war, annexed Korea and Taiwan, built modern industries, and allied itself with Britain.

The earlier Tokugawa shōgun had controlled who could buy particular types of furniture, for example in the Kansei reforms of 1789. With the Meiji Restoration, the laws were abolished and the furniture industry blossomed. The economy grew, people had more possessions to tuck away, horizons expanded, and men took up Western dress and used new articles. Families turned away from the old empty rooms, adding a veneer of Westernization.

The custom of buying furniture when marrying was pronounced. The bride's family would order a set of furnishings for the new house and two cabinet-makers would carry the chests there, swung from a pole (hence the handles). When I jokingly

---

(Previous page) Fig. 279 Ship's chest (*funadansu*) for *kitamae-bune* (coastal ships plying the Osaka–San'in–Hokkaidō route), mid-19th c., 16 x 14 x 18 in (41 x 35 x 46 cm). Photo courtesy Gomoku-dō.

Note: The author regrets that some measurements (height/length/width) are not available as pieces have been sold or have moved continent.

Fig. 280 *Meoto* (husband and wife) chest, Sendai, *keyaki* front, cedar frame, dated Meiji 40 (1907), ca. 8 ft (2.4 m) wide. Photo courtesy Kurofune Antiques.

Fig. 281 Clothing chest, Tōhoku style, *keyaki* front, 47 x 47 x 18 in (119 x 119 x 46 cm). Private Collection.

asked an old neighbor if she wanted a chest, she answered, "I'm not a bride getting married, my husband's dead of old age." In her mind, buying a *tansu* was tantamount to getting married! Nowadays, a newly married couple's goods include not only durable furniture but also electrical gadgets. They are carried to the new house on special trucks festooned with red and white bunting—the colors of good fortune—used for every inauguration in Japan.

Pointers to Dating Furniture

Writing is often found on boxes stored in warehouses or on the drawers and backs of furniture. You can be lucky and find out exactly where, when, by, and for whom a chest was made. Another way of guessing the age of furniture is to remember that the oldest iron nails were hand beaten, but by 1900 the use of round-headed, machined, Western nails had spread all round the country as they were cheaper. Rounded plank tops suggest a Taishō date.

People like to see bamboo pegs used, instead of nails, as they do not rust and appear older, but as bamboo pegs are still made, this is not an infallible guide to dating. It is also common to see bamboo pegs on most parts of a drawer, and steel nails where the front is affixed to the other wooden pieces, perhaps because it would take most strain; bamboo was free whereas nails cost money. There are also ways of knowing the age of furniture from the joinery techniques and handles. It has been well studied by foreigners, and the books in English by the Heinekens, Koizumi, Clarke, Jackson and Owen's *Japanese Cabinetry*, and the Seike translation provide a wealth of information about structures, metalwork techniques, lacquers, and regional styles of furniture.

Dealers often like to say that their goods are from the mid-Edo period. This era ran from 1603 to 1867 so that would mean about 1750, but very few pieces made then actually survive for purchase. Most clothing chests available for thousands of dollars (museum quality pieces apart) were made between 1850 and 1920. Thereafter, veneers became more common so chest durability declined, as did the aesthetic level. Although this process started twenty years earlier, Art Deco trends give zest to some veneered pieces and some late pieces were made with more care—with beveled edges to drawer fronts, for example. Also, bear in mind that customs and tastes changed at varying rates in the regions, making dating harder.

Chests (Tansu)

Tansu (chests) are very distinctive. The metalwork can be magic: fine lace on a Sado chest, gilded moons on a Yonezawa chest, repoussé ironwork on Shōnai chests, or black scrolling on a Sendai chest. The wood bears colors that Western cabinet-makers have missed. The most widely used—*keyaki* ("Oriental elm" or zelkova)—is quite unlike wood on European and American furniture, while the *shunkei* or *kijiro* lacquer finishes look so lean, it is a

Fig. 283

Fig. 284

Fig. 285

Fig. 282 Bridal chest, Yonezawa, *keyaki*, dated Meiji 31 (1898), 37 x 44 1/2 x 18 in (94 x 113 x 46 cm). Photo courtesy Kurofune Antiques.

Fig. 283 Wealthy merchant's clothing chest, Yonezawa, *keyaki*, early 19th c., 42 x 34 x 16 1/2 in (107 x 86 x 42 cm). Photo courtesy Kurofune Antiques.

Fig. 284 Bridal chest, Sendai, *keyaki* front, cedar frame, dated Meiji 41 (1908), 40 1/2 x 36 x 18 in (103 x 91 x 46 cm). Photo courtesy Kurofune Antiques.

Fig. 285 Bridal chest with double doors, Sendai, *keyaki* front and cedar frame, late 19th c., 33 x 41 x 17 1/2 in (84 x 104 x 44 cm). Photo courtesy Kurofune Antiques.

miracle the wood is not naked, yet it is very attractive and durable.

Chests were made all over the country—wherever there was wood and a market. Most pieces come from the north and east but a lot were also made in Kyūshū (those from Ōkawa are very fine) though its styles are less prized. The forests of Tōhoku and Shinshū had the best wood, and the long winters meant that men spent time indoors making something of beauty in iron and wood.

Japanese chests have strong ironwork: each corner and drawer, front and back, is guarded by iron. When moving house, the chests resist knocks. I once carried one on my car roof and unthinkingly went under a low bridge. Naturally, the chest was knocked off and landed on one corner, heavily denting it. However, the surrounding wooden panels were not seriously damaged, so the whole revived after first aid. Without the iron corner guards, disaster.

Understanding furniture requires knowledge of the woods used, so readers may refer to the table on page 177.

Fig. 287

Clothing Chests

Ishō dansu (clothing chests) come in various shapes and heights to meet changing needs. Sendai chests are usually lower, wider single pieces, 48 inches (122 cm) wide and 36 inches (91 cm) high (Figs. 284, 285), though *meoto* (husband and wife chests) like Fig. 280 may be wider. Many from other Tōhoku areas, such as Nihonmatsu and Yonezawa are of the chest-on-chest type with the two halves of roughly the same height, so separable into his and hers, or to fit side by side under a window perhaps and let in light (Figs. 282, 283).

Sado chests have resplendent overall lace-like ironwork (Fig. 287). Matsumoto chests look square and angular, while Shōnai chests have ironwork with repoussé patterns beaten out from inside, on modest wood but under beautiful black lacquer; others show attractive wood grain. Tokyo chests are plainer in color and ironwork, and more often are made of *kiri* (paulownia wood).

Unlike those in China or Korea, few Japanese chests have legs, though some later pieces have an aperture in the base, raising the chest a few inches and making for a more open look. The bottom frame may be heftier or deeper than the other structurals to protect the rest from damp. Drawer height tends to taper upwards, and there may be one or several little drawers near the lockable safe (*kinko*) built into most chests (often on the lower right). This "safe" often held family valuables and perhaps the wife's special savings. Many older chests have a secret little drawer hiding behind a shorter drawer (*kakushi*). As this was widely known, it is not surprising that burglars targeted these first!

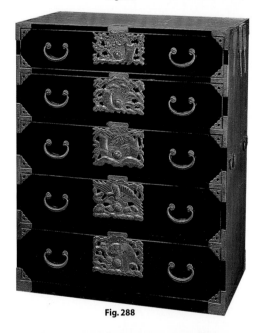

Fig. 288

Large square or U-shaped handles on the sides are common for carrying chests. Chest-on-chest types are held together by side handles. This also prevents the top moving against the bottom half when opening and closing full drawers. Fit-in handles (they can be raised for use, then hidden) suggest a twentieth-century date.

The front of a chest is always the center of attraction. Chests were not designed to be displayed to guests but were often jammed

(Opposite) Fig. 286 Chest, Yamagata, *keyaki*, ca. 1900, 46 x 48 x 17 in (117 x 122 x 43 cm). Jensen Collection.

Fig. 287 Bridal chest, Sado Island, early 20th c., 41 1/2 x 41 1/2 x 16 1/2 in (105 x 105 x 42 cm). Photo courtesy Kurofune Antiques.

Fig. 288 Shōnai chest, paulownia, ca. 1880, 42 x 35 x 18 in (107 x 89 x 46 cm). Photo courtesy Kurofune Antiques.

Fig. 289 *Kan'non-biraki* (front opening) bridal chest, North Kantō area, cedar and paulownia, 1868–80, 42 x 36 x 18 in (107 x 91 x 46 cm). Photo courtesy Kurofune Antiques.

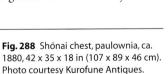

Fig. 289

Fig. 290

Fig. 290 Kitchen chest, red, black, and brown lacquered, Ōmi, late 19th c., 70 x 68 x 18 in (178 x 173 x 46 cm); Satsuma earthenware on top and dolls at side. Jensen Collection.

Fig. 291 From left: *Kan'non-biraki* clothing chest, paulownia; clothing chest divided left and right, Nihonmatsu, *keyaki*; *hibachi*, porcelain, late 19th c. Bentley Collection.

Fig. 292 *Kan'non-biraki* clothing chest, Tokyo/Suruga?, paulownia (cleaned), ca. 1900. David Pabst Collection.

Fig. 293 *Ikken-han* kitchen chest with slatted doors, Ōmi, all *keyaki*, ca. 1870, 67 x 100 x 18 in (170 x 254 x 46 cm); mammiform and dragon spouted porcelain ewers from Imari and Hirado on top; crested lacquer chest and *bingata* hanging by Cyndee Seton on left. Author's Collection.

Fig. 291

Fig. 292

Fig. 293

Fig. 295

Fig. 296

together like wall-to-wall carpeting. Sometimes they had to fit under hanging cupboards. Because only the front was visible, the sides and top were relatively neglected. Lovers of marquetry will not admire other details, such as the rather slapdash attitude to the joints (there is usually no need for special strength, unlike the beauties on *hibachi* which expand and contract daily). However, the fronts of clothing chests are often visually stunning.

The corners at the back and front are protected by iron wherever there is a danger of damage. Better pieces also have protective metal studs (*atari*) to stop damage when a handle is dropped or hiked roughly. You may see fingernail marks below handles (especially on *kiri* chests as the wood is so soft). The commonest handle shapes are the *hirute* (Fig. 282), *warabite* (Fig. 288), *kakute* (Fig. 283), *mokkō* (Fig. 292), and *gumbai* (literally "water leech, bracken, square-edged, gourd vine, and sumō fan").

The lock plates are often heavily worked. The commonest designs are auspicious emblems, such as a phoenix or groups like the crane and turtle (*tsuru-kame*), or pine, bamboo, and flowering plum (*shōchikubai*). The round locking plates of some Yamagata chests are circled by a thin band of copper alloy (*hakudō*). Because this band is shiny, foreigners suspect it is new, even if original.

Older keys were single-action (you lock by sliding the knob but unlock anti-clockwise with the key). Later double-action keys become more common (you use a key to both lock and unlock). With antique locks, you turn the key anti-clockwise to unlock with one thumb and use your other thumb to help push the knob to the left or right This is advisable as the keys are of soft metal and break easily. It makes sense not to lock them and to put the key safely away so little fingers will not play—finding a locksmith is not cheap! (A second key is great insurance.) Alternately, the keys can be rendered inoperative by taking off the lock plate and tying together the expanding element inside with wire. My cabinet-maker calls this *korosu* or "killing" the lock. Luckily, death can be undone by untying the wire! Gate and storehouse locks (*jō*) are also collectible, and an article on them appeared in *Daruma* 38.

Kan'non-biraki chests have drawers that open outwards (Fig. 289). The name comes from the little doors in front of the Kan'non (god/goddess of Mercy, depending on the perceiver) *zushi* statues common in devout homes long ago. The chests were used to store kimono and the drawers are invariably made of *kiri* to stop mold forming (Fig. 292). Often chest-on-chest, the top half had *kan'non-biraki* locking doors and the bottom had two pull-out drawers. *Kiri* develops a brownish patina which many Japanese love; others, with a mania for purity, sand it off for a pale finish.

(Opposite) Fig. 294 Kitchen chest with slatted doors, Ōmi, *keyaki* drawers, blue and white *kasuri* (*ikat*) strip on side, late 19th c., 67 x 72 x 18 in (170 cm x 183 x 46 cm); wooden cake molds on wall. David Pabst Collection.

Fig. 295 Kitchen chest with slatted doors, Ōmi, *keyaki* fronts, *hinoki* structurals, 63 x 55 x 18½ in (160 x 140 x 47 cm). Cyndee Seton Collection.

Fig. 296 Kitchen chest, Shiga Prefecture, *hinoki*, late 19th c., 67 x 48½ x 17½ in (170 x 123 x 44 cm). Photo courtesy Kurofune Antiques.

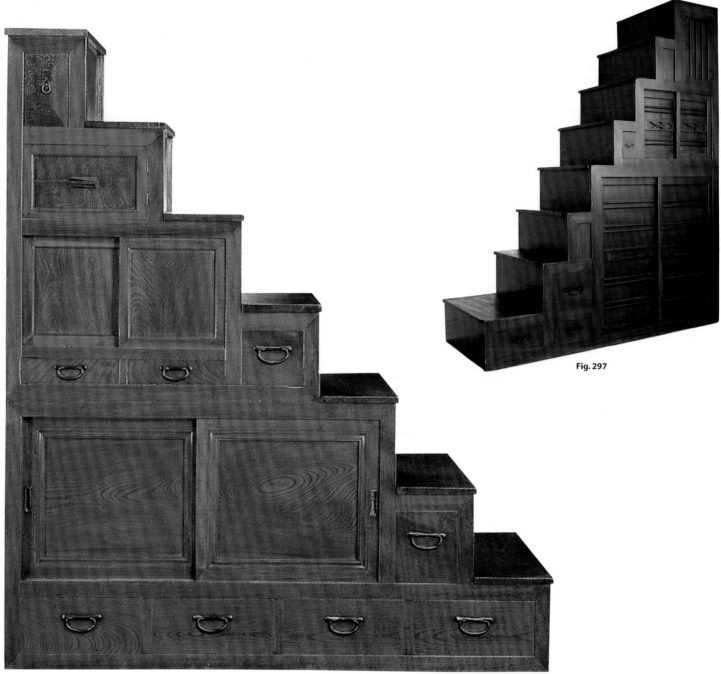

Fig. 297

Fig. 298

Kitchen Chests

Mizuya (literally "water room") is the Japanese word for a kitchen chest (Figs. 290, 293–296). They are approximately 6 ft high (183 cm) though chests from Kanazawa are a foot lower. Common widths are 3, 6, 9, and 12 feet (91, 183, 274, and 366 cm) (*sanjaku, ikken, ikken-han, niken*). The latter two are uncommon—only the rich could afford them—and made with superior materials and skill. The structurals and drawer fronts are often *keyaki*.

To make them easier to move, the top half has pegs fitting into niches on the lower half. The halves are not separable because of the pegs. Besides, the lower half has no top. A memorable adaptation in Mulroney and Lao's book shows the top half placed high against the ceiling and a food preparation space between that and the bottom half placed on the floor, with the drawers given a new top. An alternative, especially if one half is in good condition, but not the other, is to use only one piece. The lower profile allows one to put it in an entrance hall and perhaps use it for storing shoes (as a

getabako) or as an elegant, ornamental hall table.

The large storage area behind the doors often held the individual legged trays from which people ate while sitting on the floor. These came in non-stackable sets of 20–40, thus taking up a lot of room. As a *mizuya* is big, it can be turned into a drinks cabinet, bookshelf, TV or stereo area, or a dust-free display space for collectibles. The inside disappears when you close the doors—a nice trick when guests come. The drawers are handy for storage.

Mizuya with slatted doors are the pride of Ōmi, the area round Lake Biwa, but doors with one solid, often hand-sawn and perhaps recycled slab of *keyaki* are also attractive. Most drawer fronts are of superior wood, such as *keyaki*, chestnut, or box (*tsuge*). Since the doors were slid open and shut dozens of times a day, the softer wood grooves (unless given hard studs) below them tend to get worn down. This causes the door to drop, so a little strip of bamboo may be added to the top to stop it falling out. This remedy does not affect the look of a chest, so should not detract from its appeal.

Fig. 377

Fig. 378

Lacquer was extensively used to decorate male attire (horse gear and armor or sword fittings) and female ornaments like combs and hairpins. Here the market is more fragmented with a lot of goods being one-offs and history mattering as much as current appearance. Because of the strong samurai tradition honoring soldiers and their equipment, much has come down to us which serves little purpose (ancient horse girths, for example) and are not pretty either. Armor and swords are covered in another chapter.

Buddhist altars and the items that go with them (some are bronze) are beautifully lacquered and sets cost a fortune when new. The market for used altars is bedeviled by the unwillingness of Japanese to buy secondhand things. Some are exported and saved, but many altars are destroyed. Japanese connect the altars with dead relatives and the need to spend hours propitiating them with prayers and offerings, so when they move house or the grandparents die, find a reason to be rid of old associations. This means that they may be available at low cost to foreigners, but it is better to ship them overseas. Japanese would feel uncomfortable coming to your house if you had one. Given their low cost and high quality, they are a steal if you do not mind the associations!

Collecting and Care

Until three or four decades ago, lacquer was part and parcel of life in Japan and so many things remain in stores and warehouses. The mirror stand shown in Fig. 369 was part of ordinary dowries and may still turn up near you, just like writing boxes. All are intensely collectible, with their dramatic designs and low space requirements. As suggested above, lacquerware is seriously under-valued. If you are in a dry climate or have fierce heating in winter, follow the practice of museums: put the item in a cabinet and place an open bowl of water nearby to mitigate the dryness.

Avoid abrasive detergents or the use of sharp tools or blades. Wash lacquer in warm water and a little liquid soap if very dirty, and dry quickly. Normally a wipe with a wet cloth is enough. Try never to scratch the surface or peeling may later occur.

Though the day-to-day utility of lacquer has declined, its beauty remains. Great places to see lacquer are Kiyomizu San'nenzaka Museum in Kyoto, Tawara Museum in Ashiya, Japan's National Museums, the Walters Art Gallery, and the Freer Gallery, as well as Europe's great collections of Oriental Art.

CLOISONNÉ

With the current admiration for later nineteenth-century (Meiji era) work, cloisonné is very highly ranked. The technique reached an artistic and commercial climax then, whereas traditionally it had been a mere adjunct of house or sword decoration. Its commercial reign (1867–1914) was short but glorious! Thanks to advances in technique and the artistic aspirations of many leading cloisonné studios, cloisonné moved from being an artisanal activity to a branch of the fine arts.

Fig. 395a, b

History and Techniques of Sculpture

Most of Japan's great sculptures were made in the age of faith between the seventh and fourteenth centuries and are of Buddhist inspiration. Wood was the main medium, not stone, but bronze was also vital. Many would say that the country's most beautiful statue is the Buddha of the Future (Miroku) at Kōryūji, Kyoto, probably carved by a Korean immigrant in the seventh century. Jōchō, who carved the gilt wood Amida Buddha (1053) in the Byōdōin at Uji, is another admiree. Kōkei (fl. ca. 1200), his son Unkei (d. 1223), and his apprentice Kaikei were other wonderful sculptors. Kaikei's workshop probably made the 1,000-armed Kan'non and its scores of attendants in Sanjūsangendō, Kyoto.

Langdon Warner of Fogg Museum, Harvard, in *The Craft of the Japanese Sculptor*, believes that the Amida Trinity at Hōryūji "is among the most perfect and lovely bronze castings known today." It was probably made in the seventh century by Koreans who had been in Japan for several generations, evidencing Japanizing tendencies. The Tori'i sculpting family of Nara was probably of Korean origin too. Most great works are in temples and shrines or in museums, so are not easily collectible.

An ancient method of modeling involved unbaked clay that adhered to a wooden core, thanks to wisteria root fibers; the top white clay skin was brushed on like paint. Next came a gesso-like mixture with glue, and finally color. Little remains after the eighth century so perhaps the clay's weight and fragility caused sculptors to choose other media. The hollow lacquer method used a scarecrow core on which hung lacquer-soaked cloth in the appropriate shape, giving a light but strong model. Wire was added for detail

later. But there was a gradual change over to wood, which seems to have appealed to something in the Japanese craftsman's heart. At first the wood was carved and covered with fabric, but gradually the underlying knife cuts became clearer under a thin coating of preserving lacquer or color, often long since gone.

Heian and Later Currents in Sculpture

Change was inspired by the moving of the carving center from Nara to Kyoto and the arrival of new Buddhist sects or philosophies. Up to about AD 800, the images are uncomplicated figures, recognizable to ordinary people. Sakyamuni (the Buddha) is the robed figure; graceful Yakushi Nyorai is the healer; temple guardians look fierce enough to defend with ease; Miroku or Maitreya calmly waits for man to reach enlightenment so he can reach full buddhahood himself; Monju stands for wisdom; and Kan'non for mercy and sympathy. These figures were guides who could help humans towards the ideal of enlightenment.

After returning from China early in the ninth century where they had learnt the endless rituals of esoteric sects, Kōbō Daishi started the Shingon sect and Saichō the Tendai. Instead of readily graspable tenets, these sects required myriads of figures, incantations, and rituals and a whole new set of suprahuman figures with quirky qualities. Just as in India, the earliest immortals might have more than one head and many arms, now numerous divinities also required priestly interpretation and artistic expression. In reaction, ordinary people later came to rely on simple incantation to Amida and the development of paintings of paradise scenes which gave comfort, associated with Pure Land (Jōdo Shinshū) Buddhism.

(Previous page) Fig. 394 Pair of double-gourd iron vases inlaid with gold and silver with relief carvings of two-mood Daruma and *karako* (Chinese boys) haunting Hotei, Komai sei signature on inlaid plaque, Meiji era, ht 8 in (20 cm). Photo courtesy Flying Cranes Antiques.

Fig. 395a, b Buddhist altars (*zushi*). Left: Niō with many cross-like elements, perhaps *Kakure Kirishitan* (Secret Christian relic) and sword in unusual

position, wood, ht 7 in (18 cm). Right: Formerly has gilt halo, ht 5 in (13 cm). Tsuda Yoshio Collection.

Fig. 396 Seated Amida (Amitābha) in meditation, cypress wood, lacquered and gilt, mid-11th c., ht 60 in (152 cm), formerly in Sairinji, Kyoto. Photo courtesy Kyōto National Museum.

Fig. 432

Fig. 433

Fig. 434

Fig. 431 Silver dragon-spouted hot water pot/warmer/stand, body and stand with dragons in stormy seas carved in high relief, Meiji era, ht 12 in (30 cm). Photo courtesy Flying Cranes Antiques.

Fig. 432 Chased relief double-walled silver bowl with three *kirin* capering among waves, Meiji era, diam 9 1/2 in (24 cm). Photo courtesy Flying Cranes Antiques.

Fig. 433 Silver and enamel cockerel and hen (peering at spider) on a wooden stand, naturalistically carved with *shakudō*, gold, enamels, and cloisonné, signed Gyokutōsai (hen) and Issei, Meiji era, ht 9 1/2 in (24 cm). Photo courtesy Flying Cranes Antiques.

Fig. 434 Sterling silver Buddhist lion censer, Jōun signature on tablet, 19th century. Photo courtesy Flying Cranes Antiques.

(Overleaf) Fig. 435 Silver-inlaid iron stirrups (*abumi*) with red lacquer interior, Edo era. Photo courtesy Flying Cranes Antiques.

Fig. 435

Its name only surfaced in 1903 after which it exhibited widely at foreign shows until World War I. Before that, its agent, a Kyoto dealer called Ikeda Seisuke, perhaps handled its work at international or domestic exhibitions and got the credit, according to Earle, though Komai Otojirō had started selling to foreigners in Kobe in 1873. It was unusual in that the firm employed many excellent artists but stressed the company image, not individuals.

Miyao was a firm with premises in Tokyo and Yokohama specializing in portraying parcel-gilt huntsmen, actors, children playing, children with pets, family groups, etc. but mostly associated with samurai which have gilding, not inlay, for their leather, brocade, and armor lacing. It has been found that he also made beautiful ivory and wood carvings of child musicians, actors, and dancers. This discovery is surprising, given his metalworker image!

Myōchin was a famous family of metalworkers that started in the sixteenth century (Eishō era, 1504–21) by making horseshoes in Kyoto, and later *tsuba* and the skullcap part of helmets. Members gradually spread round the country, but had a large group in Tokyo. A Myōchin signature is more akin to a designer label than a personal seal. There are said to be over twenty people with that name now in Tokyo. After 1876, when swords were outlawed, they made all kinds of decorative metalwork.

Like Ikeda Seisuke, the Ōzeki Co. made a big name for itself and won many prizes, which from a modern point of view should have gone to the artisans making the works concerned. Its other name, Musashiya Co., is seen on many advertisements and pictures of Yokohama in the late nineteenth century. The father, Yahei, had been a pipe dealer but started business with his son Sadajirō shortly after Yokohama opened to foreign trade (1859). The firm handled every fashionable Meiji era item and had 24 employees in 1880.

Suzuki Chōkichi (1848–1919) used the art name Kakō. He was fond of the incense burner shape (*kōro*), low relief ornament, and expressive sculptural forms and created many great works.

Un'no Moritoshi (1834–96) came from Mito, a sword fitting center. He went to Tokyo after swords were banned and transferred those skills to vases and other ornaments. His art name was Ryōunsai.

Un'no Shōmin (1844–1915) was a pupil of Kanō Natsuo and made an Imperial Craftsman in 1896. He is known for very delicate, almost painterly, work with the chisel, providing flowing detail. He used the art name Kaiteki-an and sometimes signed off with *teppitsu*, which means "iron brush," suggesting that he felt his work had the painterly qualities of a brush artist.

Metalworkers/Firms in Meiji Japan

The following lists signatures or marks by the craftsmen and firms responsible for the flowering of Meiji metal and composite work as garnered from the Khalili Collection, dealer and auction catalogues, and other English language sources, in the hope of shedding light. With no Japanese originals available, readings and vowel lengths (vital in Japanese) may need help.

The names are in alphabetical not artistic order and may refer to firms or individuals. The terms *sei, saku,* and *zō* often follow inscriptions or signatures, and mean "made by;" *sen* = "designed by;" *kei* = "modeled by;" *teppitsu* = "incised by;" *tō'* = "carved by;" *chū* or *chūzō* = "cast by;" *koku* = "sculpted by" (also "province" or "country"); *ki* = "recorded, marked by;" *jū* = "living in;" *koi* = "copying ancient manner;" *saikusho* = "workshop."

Akasofu Gyōkō
Arthur and Bond (on a silver tea and coffee tea service presumably for a firm)

Bijitsu Seizōjō Maruki Kōjō (Maruki Art Works Factory, with address appended)
Bunkei (with Shōmin, for Hattori Clock Store, Tokyo)
Byakurō

Chikueisai Eishin
Chishinsai Katsunobu (Shinsai)
Chōkichi
Chōsai (one gold *sakazuki* is dated 1912)

Dai Nihon Kyōto jū Bunryū
Dai Nihon Teikoku Ishikawa ken

Fukuda Michiharu

Gyōkō
Gyokutōsai (carver), seal of Mitsukiyo
Gyokutōsai (hen) and Issei (cockerel) in silver on wood stand

Habiroya (in association with Kakuba Kanzaemon)
Haruaki (Watanabe Haruaki)
Hattori
Hayashi Harusada
Heian Yoyo koku, Kyoto Kuroda zō
Hideaki
Hidemitsu
Hidenao
Higashiyama Motonobu
Hira (Taira?)
Hiratsuka Mohei
Hōkyūdō Itsumin (also known for *netsuke* in wood and ivory)
Hōryūsai (made for Takasaki Kōichi)
Hōtan (one work dated 1884)

Ichiga modeled, Seijō cast, Kaneda marked this
Ichiryū Tomotoshi (1831–89)
Ichiya (real name Sekiguchi Tetsujirō, 1850–1925)
Ikkaisai Harumitsu
Ikkokusai/Mitsuyoshi
Ikkokusai (made for Tekkōdō)
Ikkokusai (=Kajima Ikkoku II, 1846–1925),
Inoue (also Kyoto Inoue)
Inshi Motonobu (who worked for the Ōzeki Co. and Imperial Household)
Ippōshi Masanori
Issa
Issei (Hasegawa Issei)

Signatures may be illegible. Alternatively, some items bear two, as different skills were applied by two artists, for example, one for the silver and another for the wood (like Hayashi and Sadayoshi respectively). Another pair on a silver piece read Sekiro and Harumasa.

Sometimes extra information is added, such as Nihon Koku Kyoto jū Komai sei (made by Komai of Kyoto, Japan, instead of Kyoto). Sometimes the same workshop wrote Nishinokyō or "western capital," as opposed to Tokyo, the eastern capital, or again Kaga no kuni Kanegawa jū Kuniyasu sei (made by Kuniyasu in Kanegawa, province of Kaga, an area round present-day Kanazawa). Another inscription is Dai Nihon Teikoku Ishikawa Ken (Ishikawa Prefecture, Japan)

Ittōsai Masatoshi (Kaneyoshi Masatoshi, 1845–1908?)
Ittōsai (Kaneyasu Masanaga)

Jomi Eisuke
Jomi Eisuke II (1839–99) (craftsman and dealer from Kyoto)
Jōun (Ōshima Jōun, 1858–1940)

Kajima Ikkoku (1846–1925)
Kajita Masuharu
Kakō chū (= cast by) art name Suzuki Chōkichi (1848–1919)
Kakuba Kanzaemon
Kaneda (Kaneda Kenjirō)
Kaneyasu Masatoshi (1845–1908?)
Kaniya Kuniharu (1869–after 1910)
Kanō Natsuo (1828-98) (one of the greats)
Katsuhika Kō (?)
Katsumitsu
Katsunori
Katsuo
Kazuo (Matsu'ura, pupil of Kanō Natsuo)
Katsura Mitsuharu (1871–1962) and Kagawa Katsuhiro (1853–1917)
Kiritsu Kōshō Kaisha (government backed firm)
Kitokuan Katsusada (Keiun)
Kōgyokusai (+ Katsuhisa seal and another for Ōzeki Co.)
Kōichi designer, Yukinari sculptor, Kiritsu Kōshō Kaisha (government export firm)
Komai (Kyoto firm, wonderful formal work, and perhaps the biggest output)
Kōnoike
Kōzan I
Kōzon
Kuninori
Kuniyasu
Kuroda
Kurokawa Eishō
Kyōto Kobayashi Shunkō
Kyōto Rakusei Yū and Kyokudō Toshichiku

Maejima Seishū
Manzeki
Maruki Kaisha (firm)
Masami (sculptor), Miyamoto (silversmith)
Masamitsu
Masatsune
Matsumura
Mitsuaki
Mitsuharu/Kagawa Katsuhiro
Miyao (also personal name Eisuke) (a favorite of many)
Miyabe Atsuyoshi

Mori
Mukai Katsuyuki
Musashiya (= Ōzeki Co.)
Myōchin (Great artists, i.e. family for generations)
Namekawa Sadakatsu (1848–post 1900)
Nemoto

Ōtake Norikuni (b. 1852), commonly found
Oyano Masayoshi (b. 1865)
Ōzeki (firm founded by Ōzeki Yahei; commissioned many works, won many prizes)
Ryōunsai, also Ryōunsai Moritoshi = Un'no Moritoshi (1834–96) (made for Ōzeki Co.)
Ryōunsai Moriyuki

Saitō Zenbei (a commissioner of craft works)
Seiji
Seikoku
Seimin (Watanabe)
Seiun, (Kanō Seiun)
Seiya
Sekiguchi Ichiya (1850–ca. 1932 and father of Shin'ya) and Kazuhiro for Tenshōdō
Sekiguchi Shin'ya (1877–ca. 1932)
Sekisai
Shōami Katsuyoshi
Shōbi
Shōun
Shōyō (Suzuki)
Sudō Seihō (also called Saiji, a student of Un'no Shōmin)
Suhōdō Hakuzen (for Marunaka firm, or Marunaka Magobei, 1830–1910)
Suzuki Chōkichi (1848–1919)

Tadakatsu and Sadakatsu (Namekawa Sadakatsu, 1848–after 1900)
Takugyokusai (Ryōyō and Ozeki)
Taiun (Yamada)
Takachika (a common signature)
Tekisui
Tomoe
Toshihiko (Nishimura 1889–1947)
Tōunsai (and Nihon no Kuni Maruki sei on mother and child figure)
Tsukada Shukyō (1848–1914)

Udagawa Kazuo (fl. 1900–10)
Un'no Moritoshi (1834–96)
Un'no Shōmin (1844–1915)
Unshō (vase with signature and Raō)

Watanabe

Yakitsugu and Kazuaki
Yamada Motonobu (1847–97)
Yamamoto Kōichi (designer), Sugiura Yukimune (engraver) for Kiritsu Kōshō Kaisha
Yosai Yamaguchi Kazuteru (1876–ca. 1930)
Yoshiaki (Yamanouchi of Mito and Edo)
Yoshimasa
Yoshimori for Tekkōdō—Un'no Yoshimori II (Bisei, 1864–1919)
Yoshinao and Tōreisai
Yoshitani
Yoshiyuki (with Masayoshi)
Yukiaki (for Nogawa Co.)
Yukinari (for Kōichi)
Yasumitsu

SWORDS AND ARMOR

The Japanese sword and its fittings are unique. Europe has valued Toledo swords for centuries but the Japanese sword is arguably finer and was revered as an object worthy of worship. The eighth-century *Kojiki* and *Nihon Shoki* place swords in the creation mythology of Japan. The Imperial regalia comprise a sword, mirror, and jewel. Blades were excavated from Kofun era (AD 300–500) burial mounds and deified; the Japanese sword has been a religious icon and had a spiritual and artistic dimension for 1200 years. Walter A. Compton, a well-known collector, says the oldest extant signed sword was made by Yukimasa in 1159.

Because of strong associations with militarism, after World War II the US wanted to get rid of Japan's swords, either by throwing them into the ocean or melting them down, but after much prevarication and some destruction finally accepted their cultural value. The fittings and armor have also long been collected.

Fig. 473

Fig. 474

Fig. 475

人
形

DOLLS

Doll collectors have a wide choice. Millennia-old traditions give dolls rich layers of physical beauty, symbolic meaning, and associations familiar to most Japanese. Doll history is part of Japanese cultural topography. *Ningyō* means "human figure," and applies to a wider variety of cultural objects than elsewhere. *Ningyō* date back thousands of years to small stone and clay figurines, mostly female, called *dōgu*, used in little understood fertility rituals before Christ. Later, kiln-fired clay figures called *haniwa* became closely associated with funerals, replacing human sacrifices. Heian era records document *hitogata* (dolls) used in funerals. Doll culture peaked in the Edo era (1603–1868)when they were made for ritual, display, and play. Beautiful messengers bring valuable insights into values, beliefs, and interests of a bygone day.

Alan Pate, of Akanezumiya, divides dolls into four categories: *hina*, which are bound up with the still-thriving Hina Matsuri or Girl's Day Festival; *gosho*, originally presentation dolls within the Imperial family; *musha*, warrior dolls linked to the former Tango no Sekku or Boy's Day Festival; and *ishō*, literally "costume" dolls, reflecting popular fads. They share common ancestors, but evolved distinct functions, structures, and associations. *Hina* and *musha* are linked to specific festivals and have purifying overtones. The *gosho* was a gift, exchanged and displayed all year, believing it brought the recipient good luck. The broad *ishō* group includes beautiful women, imitations of popular kabuki and Nō performances, specific actors, other popular culture themes, and amulets (to guard children from infection, for example).

Hina Dolls

The *hina* doll is probably the most universally recognized doll as tourist sources show images of a seated royal couple (mistakenly called "emperor and empress"), elaborately attired in "period" court costume, with attendant figures, and displayed on a tiered, red-draped stand (Figs. 477–482). Forming the central focus of the Hina Matsuri or Girl's Day Festival, held on the third day of the third month, the *hina* is Japan's most refined doll.

Yet *hina* are simple. A roughly shaped straw body is tightly covered with tailored silk brocades that give the body form. Hands are carved separately of wood and covered in a white substance known as *gofun* (crushed oyster shell and rice paste). The heads are similarly fashioned of wood or wood fiber known as *toso*, then covered in *gofun* before the features are painted on. Their long necks are inserted deep into the body. From the mid-1800s, inset glass eyes were added. Real human or silk fiber hair is arranged in traditional styles. The male (*o-bina*) clutches a scepter (*shaku*), and the female (*me-bina*) a fan.

Called the *dairi-bina* (*hina* from "the inner palace"), this royal pair represented the Imperial class, not a specific couple. Their display is seen as a visit, with food and accessory elements (*dōgu*) set out to add comfort and entertainment. Although popular attitudes have shifted over time, the *dairi-bina* were held to be temporary residences (*yorishiro*) for the spirits or gods (*kami*) who were invited during the festival to help cleanse the household and its members for the coming year.

The dolls and their retinue are brought out for display over a period of several weeks and are often joined by other categories of dolls owned by the family. Several sets may be displayed together in multi-generational households, with new sets being acquired for a girl during her first festival celebration, known as *hatsu-zekku*.

The Hina Matsuri dolls in the first decades of the Edo era resulted from pairing two separate doll forms: *amagatsu* and *hōko* (see Fig. 478). The *amagatsu* is a simple T shape composed of bundled bamboo or silk-wrapped pieces of wood. The head is a stuffed silk pouch with painted features. Either a fitted kimono made for the figure or children's clothing is draped over the body. The *amagatsu* was placed by the bedside of the child as an amulet, absorbing evil influences. A boy's dolls were burned when he came of age.

The *hōko* is more diminutive. Associated with girls, it is made of stuffed silk roughly shaped like a crawling baby with long black real or silk hair. It also served as an amulet. The strong upright *amagatsu* and more feminine *hōko* probably preceded the male/female pairing of the *dairi-bina* for Girl's Day. The earliest *hina* in the festival, called *tachi-bina* (standing *hina*), closely resemble the *amagatsu/hōko* pairing: the male figure has his arms straight out to the sides and the female has a tubular textile wrap strongly suggesting the silk-wrapped *hōko* with her diminutive arms.

The Hina Matsuri took the shape we know today during the Edo era's opening decades. Though documentary evidence is scarce, 1629 is seen as significant. A year before Princess Okiko became Empress Myōshō, at the tender age of seven (r. 1630–48), celebrations were held in her honor at the Imperial palace in Kyoto.

Fig. 477

Fig. 478

Fig. 479

Fig. 480

Her uncle, Shōgun Tokugawa Iemitsu (1603–51) sent her a puppet and a *hina* set from Edo. Kasuga no Tsubone (1579–1643), nursemaid to Iemitsu and temporarily living then in Kyoto, ordered an elaborate set of *hina dōgu* from Gotō Nuidonosuke (see Kubota Beishō's *Ningyōshi* [History of Dolls, Ningyō Makers]). This custom is said to have moved back to Edo and the shogunate upon the nursemaid's return in 1634. The ordering by Iemitsu of *hina ningyō* for his many children, and by the *daimyō* who aped him, probably spurred the growth of a *hina* market in Edo.

By the late seventeenth century, Nihonbashi was the center of Edo dolls. In Kyoto, it was along Teramachi and Shijō. Makers were appointed official suppliers to the shōgun and Imperial court in their respective cities, while others met the growing demand from merchants as well. Over time, these markets helped create new forms to keep the public interested. From the mid-1600s to the early 1800s, five distinct *hina* forms can be discerned: *kan'ei*, *kyōho*, *jirōzaemon*, *yūsoku*, and *kokin*.

Kan'ei-bina

These are named after the Kan'ei era (1624–44), when they first appeared. This was a time for stressing the dignity and long genealogy of the *daimyō* families by drawing up extensive family lists.

Kan'ei-bina were small dolls: extant examples average 5–6 inches (13–15 cm) in height. They are among the first seated *hina* (*suwari-bina*). The male and female figures wore matching textiles featuring extensive use of *kinran* (gold leaf paper lamellae). Their heads were simple with painted features over *gofun*. The hair and crown of the *o-bina* were integral to the head and painted black. A long sword was passed through the body by cutting the shelf-like trousers at the left hip, then curved sharply up behind the figure to his shoulder. Though simpler than later forms, they were considered quite luxurious at the time. *Kan'ei-bina* slowly increased in size and sophistication of face and overall shape, as the Edo era was a time of growing wealth and competition to show it by choosing more and better styles.

(Previous page) Fig. 476 *Takeda ningyō* of Taira no Tomomori (1152–85) at Battle of Dan-no-Ura (1185), when Tomomori straps second suit of armor to his back, grabs an anchor, and jumps into sea to commit suicide, early 19th c., ht 22 in (56 cm). Rosen Collection. Photo courtesy Akanezumiya.

Fig. 477 Pair of *kyōho-bina* for Hina Matsuri, late 18th c., *me-bina* (female) ht 10 in (25 cm), *o-bina* (male) ht 12½ in (32 cm), in front of *hina-byōbu* (six-panel folding screen), pigments on gold leaf, 1870–80, 15 x 37 in (38 x 94 cm). Hannig Collection. Photo courtesy Akanezumiya.

Fig. 478 Pair of *tachi-bina* (standing *hina*) for Hina Matsuri (Girl's Day Festival), 19th c., ht 9 in (23 cm). Private collection. Photo courtesy Akanezumiya.

Fig. 479 Pair of *jirōzaemon-bina* for Hina Matsuri, slightly rounder faces than normal, either made by a competitor of Jirōzaemon imitating his style, or one

referred to as *imo-bina* (potato hina), early 19th c., *me-bina* ht 13 in (33 cm), *o-bina* ht 14 in (35 cm). Carabet Collection. Photo courtesy Akanezumiya.

Fig. 480 Pair of *kokin-bina* for Hina Matsuri, mid-19th c., *me-bina* ht 13½ in (34 cm), *o-bina* ht 15 in (38 cm). Private Collection. Photo courtesy Akanezumiya.

Fig. 481

Kyōho-bina

By the Kyōho era (1716–36), a new form took center stage (Fig. 477). Keeping the basic *kan'ei-bina* silhouette but wearing sumptuous silk brocades and increasing dramatically in size, the *kyōho-bina* soon displaced it, being very popular among merchants who, by the early eighteenth century, had adopted many upper-class customs. Vying to show their new moneyed might, merchants ordered larger and larger *hina*, some near life-size—leading to government reprisals for daring to get above their station, so sumptuary laws limited the overall size, lacquer quality, and metal accessories.

Kyōho-bina are noted for their more sensitive facial carving, higher *gofun* quality, and real or silk fiber hair. Crowns and caps were separate and made of lacquer or metal. The *me-bina*'s crown became elaborate with long metal arms, dangling glass, and bead ornaments. Doll-making became more detailed.

Jirōzaemon-bina

These were named after the idiosyncratic maker who modeled this distinctive *hina* with overly rounded heads and diminutive facial features after the hook nose, dash eye (*hikime kagibana*) painting style of most artists of the Heian era (Fig. 479) (and indeed later too, *egimukyo-e*). Their textiles and body shape conveyed greater realism and conservatism than *kyōho-bina*.

Although records like the *Kyōhabutai* list a Hishiya Jirōzaemon in 1674, the *hina* form known as *jirōzaemon* did not appear until the later eighteenth century, probably due to Hinaya Jirōzaemon who the *Taisei-bukkan* listed as having shops on Muromachi in Kyoto and Nihonbashi in Edo.

Yūsoku-bina

These dolls reflect more realistically the court costumes worn by the nobility, based on rank, age, and season, in contrast to the *kyōho-bina* which is largely imaginary, designed to suggest the Imperial Court's luxury through rich brocades rather than an attempt to depict accurate dress.

The term *yūsoku* refers to an etiquette manual used by the nobility as a guide to how they should conduct their lives—what they should wear and where, restrictions on food, court rituals, terms of address, and the like.

The *yūsoku-bina* held the greatest appeal for nobles and samurai because of their correct court attire, which satisfied better their aesthetic sense. The *me-bina* wears much simpler, more subdued, layered robes and often a small metal head piece, not a crown. The male wears an overcoat based on formal, semi-formal, and informal court wear, as well as hunting attire, over a simple unlined kimono and trousers.

Kokin-bina

This is the last significant stage of *dairi-bina* development, basically intact today (Fig. 480). The term *kokin* is much debated. Some say it refers to the *Kokin-shū* poetry anthology, others to a famous Kyoto courtesan named Kokin.

Beishō suggests the kabuki actor Kokin Itarō, also of Kyoto. Now many agree with critic Saitō that the name combines "old" and "new"; the increased facial realism reflected a new aesthetic but the textiles evoked a certain apt classicism. Appearing late in the eighteenth century, they soon displaced all previous dolls.

Fig. 481 Group of *shichinin-bayashi* (musicians) for Hina Matsuri, early 19th c., ht 11 in (28 cm). Unusual rendition of seven musicians, instead of the usual five, all depicted as women, though traditionally musicians were young boys. Carabet Collection. Photo courtesy Akanezumiya.

Fig. 482 Group of *gonin-bayashi* (musicians) for Hina Matsuri, late 18th c., ht 10 in (25 cm), in front of *hina-byōbu*, pigments on silver leaf, 1870–80, 20 x 45 (50 x 114 cm). Hannig Collection. Photo courtesy Akanezumiya.

Fig. 482

Gosho Dolls

For many, the *gosho* represents the quintessential Japanese *ningyō* (Figs. 483–486). *Gosho ningyō* (palace dolls) borrow heavily from ancient aesthetic traditions. The plump child with thick black hair and brilliant white skin, often clothed in nothing more than a simple bib, is a pure expression of *wayōbi*, an aesthetic tradition based on appreciating the beauty and innocence of youth dating back to the Heian era (see Kirihata Ken's article, *Gosho Ningyō* in *The Doll: Dolls of Japan and the World*, Vol. 1). The smallish facial features on the slightly oversized head also hearken back to the purely Japanese "dash eye, hook nose" style.

Tradition says that *gosho ningyō* started in the emperor's palace in the seventeenth century as gifts conveying auspicious wishes. On their obligatory annual rounds, *daimyō* visited the court to pay respects to the emperor. *Gosho* were given to the *daimyō* in acknowledgement. Awareness of them gradually spread as the *daimyō* returned home. The direct link with the court added to their desirability and came to symbolize Kyoto court culture.

The classic shape, with its three-part division of head, body, and legs, developed over time. Its roots intertwine with the *saga ningyō* popular in the seventeenth century. Several different saga existed: religious subjects, courtesans, and ordinary townsfolk. The most celebrated depicted Chinese children (*karako*), often holding small animals. *Saga* dolls were richly ornamented with *gofun* faces and hands, thick bodies, and lacquer-decorated clothing with raised patterns and gold leaf accents. Sometimes they featured nodding heads with tongues that popped out. They were probably made by *Busshi* (Buddhist sculptors) living in Saga (near Kyoto), famed for publishing lavishly decorated books called *saga-bon* (see Kirihata Ken's article "Gosho Ningyō"). This sumptuous form probably evolved a simpler shape, the *hadaka saga* ("naked *saga*") with longer limbs and carved wood body covered with *gofun*, wearing a simple, separate silk *haragake* or bib—precursor of the *gosho*.

The basic *gosho* boy held an auspicious symbol, borrowed from classical images and associations: turtles, cranes, and peaches represented longevity (Fig. 486); *kabuto* helmets martial bravery; a treasure ship good fortune. The attribute was either part of the core, pressed tightly against the body, or separate and attached by a silk cord in more sophisticated examples. Clothing evolved from a simple bib to layered silk kimono, lacquered caps, even *tabi* socks.

Standing figures followed, enlarging the bounds of expression (Fig. 483). The Edo era saw great artistic output in nearly all fields. Theater particularly saw spectacular growth and popularity. Nō, kabuki, puppet *jōruri*, and mechanical puppet theater were all successful. *Mitate* (parody) *gosho* forms soon developed. Images drawn from popular kabuki or Nō plays appeared in *gosho* form, either single figures or elaborate tableaux with many images. A simple signature attribute or prop allowed patrons to identify the play or story in question, often made even more popular by the dissemination of woodblock prints featuring actors in their famous roles.

Perhaps taking their cue from the successful mechanical puppet (*karakuri ningyō*) theaters of the day, *karakuri gosho* were also made: seated gosho figures with hollowed interiors, pivoting arms (and occasionally, heads) allowed arms to be raised and lowered to place masks on the face, or provide a dancing motion, just by turning a knob at the back (Fig. 484).

The earliest *gosho ningyō* were of carved *kiri* (paulownia) wood, usually from a single block, covered with layers of fine *gofun* and burnished to create a shiny, porcelaneous effect. The simple features were stressed with *sumi* ink. The gift-giving aspect of *gosho* could be enhanced by painting a red *mizuhiki* (presentation ribbon) on the forehead. Appropriate human or silk fiber hair was added. Later forms employed *toso* wood composite, *papier mâché*, or even clay for the base shape to reduce cracking over time.

By the late eighteenth century, artists had great technical expertise in creating triple-jointed (*mitsuore*) dolls allowing standing, sitting, or kneeling positions. The addition of flexible silk crepe upper arm joints also allowed for easy costume changes. This began the shift within the *gosho* category away from purely display dolls to a range of sophisticated play dolls and the celebrated *ichimatsu ningyō* of the mid-nineteenth century—still one of the most popular forms.

Fig. 483

Fig. 483 Standing *gosho ningyō* wearing an overcoat of typical 18th c. textile, inscription on lining reading "Seeker of Truth," late 18th c., ht 18 in (46 cm). Lapin Collection. Photo courtesy Akanezumiya.

Fig. 484 Seated *karakuri* (mechanical) *gosho ningyō* with mask of Daikoku, god of daily wealth, *papier mâché*, early 19th c., ht 9 in (23 cm). Ayervais Collection. Photo courtesy Akanezumiya.

Fig. 485 Seated *karakuri* (mechanical) *gosho ningyō* now wearing mask of Daikoku, god of daily wealth, *papier mâché*, early 19th c., ht 9 in (23 cm). Ayervais Collection. Photo courtesy Akanezumiya.

Fig. 486 Pair of *gosho ningyō* with peach blossoms, dated Kyōwa 2 (1802), ht 6 in (15 cm). Ayervais Collection. Photo courtesy Akanezumiya.

Fig. 484

Fig. 485

Fig. 486

Musha Dolls

The peace of the Edo era followed centuries of internecine warfare that had inhibited the country's growth and prosperity. The Tokugawa shōgun, with their headquarters in Edo, forcibly united the country under the 260-year *pax Tokugawana*. The samurai families who had fought for centuries were now the ruling class and operated the bureaucracy. Deprived of wars (their *raison d'être*), samurai had to adjust to their new status, rapidly changing economic realities, and great social dislocations. During the opening decades of the Edo era, nostalgia for war found many expressions, including the re-emergence of Tango no Sekku, celebrating boys in the fifth month, as the third month Hina Matsuri did for girls.

With roots dating back to China where mugwort was hung from the eaves to repel disease, Tango no Sekku was feted as early as the Heian era when courtiers tied iris leaves (*shōbu*) to their caps to ward off evil. The likeness of the iris leaf to a sword lent martial overtones, with displays of arrow shooting, while evil spirits were driven away by beating the ground with bunches of iris leaves.

Edo era Tango no Sekku changes can be traced through woodblock prints. Old military households tied iris leaves to their house eaves in the time-honored way and displayed standards and military banners on the street outside. Children held mock battles using iris leaves as swords, engaging in the old ritual for driving away evil. Weapons and other symbols of the samurai's glory days were displayed. Helmets crafted entirely of iris leaves were mounted on poles, and by the 1670s small *ningyō* were tied over helmets portraying figures from the martial past.

Edo's *ningyō* shops soon featured free-standing doll heroes. The lasting popularity of warrior tales (*gunki monogatari*) recounting battles between the Taira and Genji clans in the twelfth century, as well as more recent tales, provided heroes and tragic figures. In the late seventeenth century, Tango no Sekku displays gradually moved indoors and *ningyō* took on greater importance. More privacy allowed merchant households to join in.

Though the historical and legendary personages the *ningyō* artist could draw on from Japan's long history seems limitless, six core figures emerged during the Edo era: Empress Jingū and her minister Takenouchi no Sukune (Fig. 487); Minamoto no Yoshitsune (Fig. 493); Benkei and Ushiwakamaru at the Gojō Bridge (Figs. 489, 491); Toyotomi Hideyoshi (Figs. 488, 492); Katō Kiyomasa (Fig. 494); and, in the early Meiji era, Emperor Ōjin (Fig. 490). From these figures, boys were taught about valor and the qualities they embodied, and were urged to emulate them.

Jingū kōgō

Empress Jingū, shaman and military heroine, is a fascinating figure. Through most of Japanese history, she was considered an actual woman but is now a composite figure, mostly myth and legend. Her tale centers on conquering the Korean Peninsula in AD 200 or thereabouts as this is mostly myth. Leading the Japanese armada with faithful minister Takenouchi at her side, and utilizing

Fig. 487

the powerful tide-shifting gems given by Ryūjin, dragon king of the sea, Jingū subjugated the Koreans without bloodshed through a show of superior culture and divine favor. The twist to the story comes with the revelation that Jingū was pregnant at the time. To delay the birth, she tied a girdle of rocks around her womb, ultimately carrying baby Ōjin for 19 months before finally giving birth on her triumphant return to Japanese soil in 201.

Jingū is the only female in the Boy's Day display (Fig. 487). She usually stands in a suit of armor over rich silks. Atop her head is a tall, lacquered cap, at her side a long sword covered with tiger pelts. She carries a bow in her hand and a full quiver of arrows on her back. At first glance, she appears male, but long black hair trails down her back. Her teeth are also blackened as a sign of beauty, and she sports aristocratic "sky brows" painted high on her forehead, indicating her nobility and gender. Takenouchi, vassal and advisor, kneels at her side cradling the baby Ōjin. His face, wizened with wrinkles and folds, sports a long white beard and moustache, and bushy white eyebrows.

Yoshitsune

Minamoto no Yoshitsune (1159–89) is the quintessential tragic hero, lionized and honored. A brilliant tactician and fearless leader of the Genji, Yoshitsune carved a brilliant but short arc in Japanese history. After defeating the Taira clan in a series of fights during the Gempei Wars, and betrayed by his older half-brother Yoritomo, Yoshitsune lived his last years as a fugitive, ultimately committing suicide in the far north, hounded by his brother's troops.

Yoshitsune is central to Boy's Day (Fig. 493). He usually sits on a campstool with lacquered paper armor and heavy helmet featuring a large dragon prow, an emblem repeated on his breastplate. At his side is a long sword and bow, at his back a quiver, and in his right hand a *saihai* (battle whisk) or *gumbai* (military fan), showing that he is the commander. Kneeling at his side, a vassal often holds aloft the white Genji banner.

Musashibō Benkei and Ushiwakamaru

To explain Yoshitsune's brilliance as a general, legends grew up about his youth, of the magic mountain *tengu's* secret training of Ushiwakamaru (his childhood name), and various journeys and adventures. The most popular recounts his fateful encounter with the warrior monk Benkei (Fig. 489) one moonlit night on Gojō Bridge in Kyoto. The great warrior monk Musashibō Benkei (d. 1189), despairing of ever finding a worthy master to serve, consulted a soothsayer who foretold that he would find his destiny after capturing a thousand swords. In his quest, Benkei stationed himself at night on the Gojō Bridge and challenged passers-by, summarily defeating them. One night on the bridge, he meets Ushiwakamaru, then serving as a court page. Armed only with a fan, the youth nimbly outmaneuvers Benkei and defeats him, earning Benkei's unwavering allegiance.

Fig. 488

Fig. 489

Fig. 487 *Musha ningyō* set of Empress Jingū, Takenouchi no Sukune holding baby Ōjin, and bannerman, for Boy's Day Festival, mid-19th c., ht 24 in (61 cm). Rosen Collection. Photo courtesy Akanezumiya.

Fig. 488 *Musha ningyō* of Toyotomi Hideyoshi (1536–98) for Boy's Day Festival, early 19th c., ht 14 in (35 cm). Hannig Collection. Photo courtesy Akanezumiya.

Fig. 489 *Musha ningyō* of Musashibō Benkei (d. 1189) for Boy's Day Festival, ca. 1800, ht 12 in (30 cm). Rosen Collection. Photo courtesy Akanezumiya.

Fig. 490 *Musha ningyō* set of Emperor Ōjin, Takenouchi no Sukune, and bannerman, 1880–1900, emperor ht 15 in (38 cm). Private Collection. Photo courtesy Akanezumiya.

Fig. 490

Fig. 491

Fig. 492

Fig. 493

Woodblock print images of this scene abound. From the fourteenth century, Nō performances also enacted this drama. Such *ningyō* appear as early as 1688. Ushiwakamaru atop a bridge stanchion with only a fan faces Benkei with a long halberd and arsenal of weapons strapped to his back, his shaven face and grimacing features a marked contrast to Ushiwakamaru's noble youth (Fig. 491).

Toyotomi Hideyoshi

The historical Toyotomi Hideyoshi (1536–98) is credited with ending centuries of civil conflict. His strong-handed tactics and military campaigns brought to heel the competing *daimyō*.

Hideyoshi *ningyō* almost always sit cross-legged, clothed in silk brocades overlaid with lacquered paper armor, a paulownia crest prominent on the breastplate (Figs. 488, 492). Never helmeted, he either wears a black lacquered *eboshi* or signature Chinese-style cap with flaring wings. He holds a folded fan in his right hand.

Katō Kiyomasa

Like Musashibō Benkei, Katō Kiyomasa (1562–1611) is an *aramusha* or rough warrior, celebrated as Hideyoshi's vassal and for his exploits in Korea. He proved a popular Boy's Day image and is seen slaying tigers, seated as a military commander on a camp stool, or kneeling, showing he obeys Hideyoshi. Kiyomasa dolls started appearing in the early nineteenth century, largely coinciding with those depicting Hideyoshi. Although figures of Hideyoshi and Kiyomasa were often paired, each also existed independently.

Kiyomasa is readily identified. He has exaggeratedly fierce facial features, and his hair is usually long at the sides to stress his tough, wild nature (Fig. 494). Between 1840 and 1880, in particular, the *gofun* was often tinted to give a rougher look. Kiyomasa sports an almost conical tall helmet—his signature—with a giant circular crest repeated on his breastplate. When seated on a campstool, he typically holds a battle whisk and a long sword covered with tiger pelt at his hip. (Legend says he battled a tiger in Korea.)

Emperor Ōjin

With the Meiji Restoration of 1868, Japan saw a radical shift in social structure. Merchants were no longer at the bottom of the social ladder, samurai could soon carry their swords in public no more, and the emperor moved from Kyoto to head the government in Edo (now Tokyo). The emperorship was newly burnished and greater priority given to imagery supporting it. Traditional samurai images began to give way to ancient Imperial figures and even images of Emperor Meiji himself.

The sudden inclusion of Emperor Ōjin as a central icon at Boy's Day reflects this shift. Ōjin had long been an infant with his mother and cradled in Takenouchi's arms, but now a warrior, seated on a campstool, in lacquered paper armor with a battle fan in his right hand (Fig. 490). No crest is officially associated with Ōjin, but his armor often bears a sun and moon motif at the neck. Like

Fig. 494

Hideyoshi, he rarely has a helmet, but sports instead a lacquered *eboshi*. His face is youthful. Ōjin's arrival coincided with the use of inset glass eyes, and most Ōjin figures, even the earliest, use this technology new to doll making.

Ishō Dolls

Ishō ningyō (fashion or costume dolls) represent the broadest category: play dolls with exchangeable wigs, dramatically posed theatrical figures, *mitate* or parody tableau dolls featuring stories from the past, and talismanic figures like the *hōsō ningyō* (measles protection dolls) placed by a child's bed to ward off measles and smallpox demons. Not associated with any specific festival, *ishō ningyō* were given and displayed throughout the year. Just as woodblock prints help to trace cultural trends during the Edo era, *ishō* give valuable insights into shifting clothing styles, popular theatrical pieces, interest in Japan's past, even health practices and beliefs.

Fig. 491 *Musha ningyō* set of Musashi-bō Benkei and Ushiwakamaru on Gojō Bridge, ca.1900, Benkei ht 12 in (30 cm), bridge 21 x 45 x 12 in (53 x 114 x 30 cm). Rosen Collection. Photo courtesy Akanezumiya.

Fig. 492 *Musha ningyō* of Toyotomi Hideyoshi for Boy's Day Festival, early 19th c., ht 10 in (25 cm). Private collection. Photo courtesy Akanezumiya.

Fig. 493 *Musha ningyō* of Minamoto no Yoshitsune (1159–89) on campstool, dragon prow on helmet, and crest on breastplate, 19th c., ht 16 in (41 cm). Private collection. Photo courtesy Akanezumiya.

Fig. 494 *Musha ningyō* of Katō Kiyomasa (1562–1611) showing exaggerated features of an *aramusha* (rough warrior) figure, 19th c., ht 16½ in (42 cm). Rosen Collection. Photo courtesy Akanezumiya.

Fig. 495

Fig. 496

Unlike *hina* or *musha* dolls—figures frozen in the past, with few changes in clothing and posture—*ishō ningyō* were fluid, quickly reflecting shifts in clothing or taste. The *bijin ningyō* (beautiful woman dolls) best indicate this aspect (see page 2 and Figs. 495, 497, 498). *Bijin* were popular throughout the Edo era, with its overwhelming emphasis on the pleasure districts and its courtesans of the *ukiyo* (floating world). *Saga*-type *bijin ningyō* can be found from the early seventeenth century, accurately depicting textile patterns, hairstyles, and even comb placement. *Ishō*-style *bijin* in other doll forms followed. The earlier trend of carved or formed hair indicative of the *saga* style gave way to elaborately coiffed real or silk fiber hair, and thus greater realism. New textile arts such as *yūzen*, where a pattern is mapped out in paste resist before dyeing, are readily seen in doll kimono from the late seventeenth century. Beauties could be included in expanded displays for the doll festival but were appreciated for their inherent appeal and were thus displayed any time.

Edo era books often mention *ningyō* in conjunction with dramas, the stories that inspired them, and their actors. Dolls were directly linked with two main early Edo era theatrical arts: *jōruri* (*bunraku*) (Fig. 496) and the mechanical puppet theater (*karakuri ningyō*) founded in 1662 and made famous by Osaka's Takeda family. *Ningyō* artists were quick to exploit the popularity of these

stories, riding on the back of widespread distribution of illustrated books and *ukiyo-e*.

Takeda ningyō symbolize the dolls created in response to theater culture (Figs. 496, 499, 501). Mounted on black lacquered bases representing a stage, they usually appear in dynamic, half twisting poses, their heads tilted slightly, one leg on a prop central to the story, their faces contorted with emotion and frequently bearing the painted lines of the *kumadori* make-up made famous by the Danjūrō family of kabuki actors, their eyes locked in a dramatic *mie*, crossed and fixed in a moment of intense realization—the high point of a kabuki play. Termed *yakusha* (actor) or *kabuki ningyō* in Edo era literature, the modern name *takeda* comes from Osaka's Takeda theaters, popular during the first half of the eighteenth century although their exact origins are unknown. Takeda *ningyō* were popular until about 1850–60.

Takeda dolls are as aggressive and wild as the *gosho* are soothing, but are hard to come by. Benkei and Yoshitsune might be shown in fighting stances, while *kataki-uchi* or "blood revenge" stories from the 47 Rōnin and Soga Brother sagas were popular, as well as folktales and legends such as Urashima's adventures with the Dragon Princess under the sea. Tarō is often shown standing among the waves, carrying a box containing Time itself.

Fig. 495 *Ishō ningyō* of Yōkihi (Yang Kuei-fei), celebrated 8th c. Chinese beauty whose involvement with the Chinese emperor led to civil war, early 19th c., ht 12 in (30 cm). Ayervais Collection. Photo courtesy Akanezumiya.

Fig. 496 *Ishō ningyō* depicting "Arrow Sharpening Scene" from kabuki play *Yanone*, late 18th c., ht 19 in (48 cm). Ayervais Collection. Photo courtesy Akanezumiya.

Fig. 497 *Mitsuore* (triple-jointed) *bijin ningyō* interchangeable wig doll (*katsura-gae ningyō*) depicted kneeling surrounded by her wigs, late 19th c., ht 16 in (41 cm). Carabet Collection. Photo courtesy Akanezumiya.

Fig. 497

Fig. 498

Fig. 498 Pair of *mitsuore bijin*, one standing, demonstrating the Edo era *mitsuore's* ability to balance while standing, one kneeling, early 19th c., standing ht 10½ in (27 cm), kneeling ht 6 in (15 cm). Ayervais Collection. Photo courtesy Akanezumiya.

Measles or "Illness Prevention" Dolls

The measles doll is a very rare and little understood *ishō ningyō*. It depicts the fiery red face and long, flaming red hair of a *shōjō* standing with a saké cup in one hand and a giant ladle in the other (Figs. 500, 502, 503). *Shōjō* were mythical creatures that lived in the sea and were partial to saké. Red has traditionally been a lucky color in Japanese society because it attracted evil influences and drew them away. The red of *hōsō ningyō* was believed to attract the *hōsōgami* (measles demon). Similarly *hōsō-e* (measles pictures), painted red and posted on doorways and in sick rooms, were talismans guarding a child. Though usually crafted of clay or *papier mâché*, some *hōsō ningyō* display the fine techniques of *ishō ningyō* popular in the eighteenth century. They have well-formed features (usually laughing), covered in a red-tinted *gofun*. Their red-dyed silk fiber hair flows down to their waists, and their bodies are clothed in rich brocades. Frequently, they have elaborate stands like *takeda ningyō*.

Bunraku Dolls

Puppets (*ayatsuri ningyō*) can trace their origins to Shintō shrines where they were used in sermon play-stories to illustrate religious topics. *Kugutsushi* or traveling puppeteers carried this tradition to the country and put on secular dramas for farming and fishing folk.

By 1780, more permanent theatres had been set up in Osaka for puppet dramas accompanied by *jōruri* narration and music. The term *bunraku* comes from the Bunraku-za, founded in 1872 and named after a famous performer of the period, Uemura Bunrakuken. Immensely popular, *bunraku* developed into a significant art form. The most talented artisans crafted the head, hands, and feet of wood, delicately painting in the features, then adding hair and other features. Textiles, rich and sumptuous, accurately portray the garb of the period.

Bunraku dolls are dynamic, with articulated arms, hands, and fingers, heads that twist at the neck, eyes that can open and shut and even move side to side, as eyebrows lift and furrow. The figures come to life and dramas unfold at the hands of the puppeteer.

Historical plays called *jidaimono* draw from warrior tales and focus on samurai and the upper strata of society, while *sewamono* or domestic plays deal with ordinary people. They served as morality plays and provided direct social commentary on their life and times. Plays like *Hade Sugata Onna Maiginu*, where a husband leaves his wife for a courtesan and ends in the lovers' double suicide, with their child being left in the care of the wife, serve as a reminder of the fate of those going against the mores of the time.

Ichimatsu

Ichimatsu dolls are said to be named after Sanogawa Ichimatsu, a kabuki actor in Edo, popular during the Genbun and Kampo eras (1736–43) (Fig. 504). Ichimatsu played teenager roles and was an idol for women, so they focused on his clothes.

The *ichimatsu moyō* (pattern) *hakama* (divided skirt for men) with a stone pavement design worn by Ichimatsu on stage was much sought after, becoming the favored pattern for dolls and young women. When dolls aping his face were put on sale, his fans made a dash for them. Girl dolls often had their hair bobbed short while the hair on boy dolls was painted with a brush. Girl dolls were more popular than boys (80 percent of all *ichimatsu* dolls were girls) and most are 7–23 inches (18–58 cm) tall.

Fig. 499

Fig. 500

Fig. 501

Ichimatsu is a general term for cuddly dolls made of molded sawdust with movable arms and legs. Their arms, legs, and face are inserted into a body. When parents married off a daughter, they gave her an *ichimatsu* doll, hoping it would always be a good, uncomplaining friend, as wifehood at that time was likely to entail great hardship given women's low social position. Wives were expected to perform most of the chores in a house, getting up first, going to bed last, even while caring for their children. A wife was under the thumb of her mother-in-law who bossed her around unmercifully if she happened to have been trained differently or was in any way careless, insufficiently clean, or disrespectful.

These dolls used to be called *hadaka* (naked) *ningyō*. An eighteenth century *e-hon* (picture book) says "It is a filial duty to cherish and prevent damage to a hadaka *ningyō* given by parents." They were often sold naked so a mother could make clothes for them in front of her daughters, thereby teaching them the basics of dressmaking. At other times, the clothes could be taken off so that children could play at dressing them.

Sode (sleeve) *ichimatsu* or *mame* (miniature) *ichimatsu* dolls often appear in doll galleries. Their height varies from 0.5 to 6 inches (1 to 15 cm). They were made from the Meiji period (1868–1912) onward, and were particularly common in the period from 1926 until 1935. Because *sode ichimatsu/mame ichimatsu* are so small, they fade away in the presence of Girls' Day, warrior or regular *ichimatsu* dolls, unless displayed in large groups, so care is needed when collecting such dolls to maintain a balance of size and numbers for display.

Kokeshi Dolls

These lathe-turned wooden dolls were probably started in the Bunka-Bunsei eras (AD 1804–29) in Tōhoku (northeast Japan) by farmers and sold mostly at the spas so popular there. *Kokeshi* may have started with a farmer's wishes for good harvests or a family, and later were given for comfort to women who had miscarriages or lost babies. *Kokeshi* were probably made in the long nights of the snow-bound winters from timber like maple, dogwood, and magnolia for which there was no cash market.

At first tools were primitive, then pulley lathes came in; the wife pulled and the husband applied the blade to the wood. Color was applied as the doll (and sometimes other toys like tops) turned on the spindle. Later came kick lathes and, finally, mechanical lathes. Japanese collectors prefer the older *kokeshi* dolls from before this (post-war) turn.

When the United States Army occupied Japan, many soldiers' wives sought out *kokeshi*, finding them cute, and turners (often in towns near Tokyo, not Tōhoku) became more creative, turning out non-traditional shapes for them and for tourist sites all over Japan, such as aubergines (*nasu*) at Nasu, Tochigi, *kokeshi*-headed toothpicks for eating Japanese cakes, or the Seven Lucky Gods in all kinds of outlandish outfits (Fig. 506).

Doll Types and Sizes

Kokeshi dolls have been divided by origin into Tsuchiyu, Yajirō, Tōgatta, Narugo, Hijiori, Sakunami, Zaō, Kijiyama, Nambu, and Tsugaru "strains," though the individualizing traits may get mixed due to travel and commerce. Dolls could be made in one piece or two, when the head was separate and sometimes glued into the body or could swivel or nod.

Adults started collecting *kokeshi* in the 1920s, leading to an increase in sizes from tiny to immense. Up until then, the standards for children's play were 5, 7, and 10 inches (13, 18, and 25 cm) high. According to Itske Stern, who provided the facts in this section, attractive dolls should have good character, shape, and color.

■ The body should have a balanced shape and the head not be top-heavy.

■ Facial features should be lively and applied with a calligraphy brush.

■ Patterns on the body and head should be positive, not hesitant. They need not be even, but they should be typical of the doll strain.

■ Color balance should be pleasing and not watery-looking. Greens and violets fade first.

The value of the doll comes from the above four features and the artist's popularity and craftsmanship.

Well-known doll makers who have turned out attractive dolls include Sakurai Shōji and Itō Shōichi in Naruko; Ni'iyama Hisashi and Satō Yoshizō (late father) and Fumio (son) in Yajirō; and Suzuki Shōji and Satomi Matsuhiro at Yamagata.

Fig. 502

Miscellaneous Dolls

Kimekomi dolls were originally made of willow wood at the Kamo Shrines in Kyoto in the 1730s. They had grooves into which textiles were fitted to keep their line and lend a smart appearance.

Hakata dolls date from 1620–30 and were made in Hakata, northern Kyūshū. Made of clay, they stress not clothes but realistic features and gestures, without being dressed up.

Imada dolls come from the eponymous district of Tokyo and are made from rough earthenware, often in the shape of animals, but they may promise love or request good fortune.

Kobe dolls were made in that city from the late nineteenth century. They included black men or ghoulish figures whose tongues came out or cut open watermelons or poured saké (Fig. 505). They were modeled after *bunraku* dolls and were very popular with Western tourists till World War II, but too dear for Japanese. As a

---

Fig. 499 *Takeda ningyō* standing by well, early 19th c., ht 22 in (56 cm). Thomas Collection. Photo courtesy Akanezumiya.

Fig. 500 *Hōsō ningyō* (measles prevention doll), talisman against measles and smallpox, depicting red-faced *shōjō* (mythical ape), early 19th c., figure ht 12 in (30 cm). Ayervais Collection. Photo courtesy Akanezumiya.

Fig. 501 *Takeda ningyō* of Toyotomi Hideyoshi (1536–98), early 19th c., ht 33 in (84 cm). Ayervais Collection. Photo courtesy Akanezumiya.

Fig. 502 Detail of red-faced *hōsō ningyō*, early 19th c., ht 12 in (30 cm). Ayervais Collection. Photo courtesy Akanezumiya.

Fig. 503

result, many collections were formed in America and Europe, but a Japanese has founded a Toy Museum an hour from Kobe with many outstanding examples (see *Daruma* 34).

Tsutsumi and *Hanamaki* dolls are all made of clay and represent *kyōdo ningyō*, that is, the dolls made all over Japan by nonspecialists. Normally their quality does not match sophisticated Kyoto dolls.

Maneki Neko (beckoning cats) are less dolls for children, more amulets for stores, as the cat beckons passers-by to come in and eat or buy things (see *Daruma* 11). *Papier mâché*, wood, stoneware, iron, and painted clay are common materials. In most cases, the left paw is raised chin or ear high but there are righties too.

Local craftsmen make special things everywhere. Every year Kameidō Shrine in Tokyo sells 20,000–30,000 wooden bullfinches (*uso*, or the Japanese for "fib") of various sizes that may bring better luck in the New Year. Similarly, a common souvenir in Tōhoku is an eagle with carved tail feathers. Ainu carvers also make bears and fish for Hokkaidō tourists.

Collecting Dolls

In the words of Alan Pate, who provided much of the material for this chapter and is an acknowledged authority in this field (see *Daruma* 14 and 17), "Collecting antique Japanese *ningyō* can be rewarding. The wide variety of figures created and their deep underlying meanings provide an endless array of pursuits. Though daunting at first, the vocabulary and forms of the dolls are easily mastered and invaluable in evaluating and understanding Japanese dolls. Unlike many other Japanese art forms, *ningyō* remain affordable, and the novice collector can still find excellent examples dating back to the 18th century. Like any other art form, basic knowledge of their history, construction techniques and imagery will go a long way in helping collectors in their quest."

High standards of doll-making have long reigned in Japan. The nineteenth century saw chrysanthemum dolls formed of live flowers, and in the twentieth century, doll artists Hirata Gōyō, Hori Ryūjo, and Kagoshima Jūzō were made Living National Treasures.

Fig. 503 *Hōsō ningyō*, early 19th c., figure ht 8½ (22 cm). Carabet Collection. Photo courtesy Akanezumiya.

Fig. 504 Kneeling *Ichimatsu ningyō*, ca. 1900, ht 35½ in (90 cm). Goldberg Collection; with standing *gosho ningyō*, 19th c., ht 16 in (41 cm). Rosen Collection. Photo courtesy Akanezumiya.

Fig. 505 Kobe dolls, late 19th c. Photo courtesy Oriental Treasure Box.

Fig. 506 Collection of *kokeshi* dolls, 20th c. Photo courtesy Itske Stern.

Fig. 504

Fig. 505

Fig. 506

FLOWER BASKETS

It is very easy to be dismissive of baskets if you come from a background where baskets were used for gardening or shopping, without much concern for their appearance (beyond perhaps an awareness that a handmade basket was preferable to a store-provided shopping bag with which you advertise—for free!—some vile goods, or even worse, a plastic bag that depletes fossil fuels, warms the world, and despoils the sea). Yet, the awareness of flowers and their containers among Zen followers, Tea masters, and Ikebana adepts brought about a major change. After centuries of mere utilitarian use and aesthetic neglect or blindness, flower baskets (often following bronze models) became a part of human life where form, materials, and a measure of masterliness combined to produce works we humans can be proud of.

It is perhaps only a century plus a few decades that the art basket movement and wide appreciation of basket masters started, but ever since Lloyd Cotsen exhibited his incredible collection and published the deluxe book, *Contemporary Japanese Baskets: Masterworks of Form and Texture*, Japanese flower arrangement baskets (*hanakago*) have achieved star status: attractive pieces by famous names fetch thousands of dollars.

Historical Background

Baskets dating from the late Jōmon era (AD 2–3 c.) have been found at shell mounds in Shinpukuji, Saitama, and Torihama, Fukui Prefecture. Jōmon potters displayed great skill in plaiting patterns. The first basket found was shallow and mat-plaited, with narrow bamboo strips and a thickly lacquered surface. Others were un-lacquered, though lacquered ones were often twill-plaited.

The Shōsōin repository (AD 756) houses hundreds of plain and shallow bamboo baskets with no handles. They may be foreign and have held flower petals for scattering at religious ceremonies.

Baskets for collecting crops, or leaves for sericulture, are age-old but have not usually survived the ravages of time. However, Tea culture from China started spreading among Zen priests from the late twelfth century, then among warriors like Ashikaga Yoshimasa (1436–90), the eighth shōgun, who is credited with being the first to use a bamboo basket for non-religious flower arranging. After the tea ceremony and flower arrangement movements became central to cultured life in the sixteenth century, flower baskets became connoisseurs' items. Most were modeled on Chinese bronzes. According to Anita Meyer (*Daruma* 36), "These early Chinese baskets (*karamono* or Chinese objects) are identifiable by their

Fig. 508